Something
ABOUT THE
BLOOD

KOLA O. EMIOLA

SOMETHING ABOUT THE BLOOD

© 2016 KOLA EMIOLA

ISBN: 978-978-54202-1-0

Published by:
Gintzprince Limited
gintzprinceltd@yahoo.com

For further information please contact

Nigeria Address:
Dominion Impact Church,
G.P.O. Box 37765, Dugbe, Ibadan,
Oyo State, Nigeria.
Mobile: +2348023533705
Email: deccnig2@yahoo.com
website: www.dominionimpactchurch.org

USA Address:
Dominion Impact International Church,
P.O. Box 98794, Seatle, W. A. 98198.
website: www.dominionimpactchurchusa.org

Contents

Dedication

I want to dedicate this book to you my friend that is called "nobody" now, that after reading this, will rise with the truth contained in it and become "somebody" that will affect generations for our king.

And principally this book is dedicated to the Maker and the Lifter of men. Thank you for making and lifting someone like me to write these pages. I am forever grateful to you Jesus my Saviour and Lord.

Acknowledgment

Bola, you are the perfect match for my strength and weakness. Thank you for believing in me and standing by my side through this adventure, even when it looks uncertain and not too clear. Thank you for stepping out from what you know and comfortable with for the sake of Jesus and the Gospel. If the sun refuses to shine I will still love you my friend.

And I like to thank all our leadership team. I am so grateful for having these addicted lovers of Jesus Christ. You are the best any man will ever dream to have around him. Your commitment to God and to our common assignment is indeed encouraging all the time. Your uncommon support and undivided loyalty noticeable through all the pages of this book. The writing of this book is truly a team effort. And all at Dominion Impact Church my heart goes out to you saying thank you.

I am blessed to be the Pastor of this uncommon church, you are indeed great.

Endorsement

In "Dynamics of the Life in the Blood" Pastor Kola Emiola captures the significance of the Precious Blood of Jesus Christ in the day-to-day life of the believer. With clarity and economy of words he tells us what the Blood is, what it has accomplished and, most importantly to us, how to appropriate it in our daily walk. In his warm and inviting way, Pastor Kola outlines the power that is overlooked or neglected by most Christians and brings us to a place where we do not want to live another minute without the Miracle Working Blood. You will want to read this book on a regular basis to supercharge your walk with the Lord. I know I will.

Rev. Randy Emerson,
Senior Pastor,
Cloverdale Church, Surrey, British Columbia, Canada

The Bible says in Revelation 12:11 "And they overcame him by the blood of the Lamb and by the word of their testimony." In Kola Emiola's book There is Something About the Blood Kola lays a clear foundation and brings fresh revelation for the Believer to be equipped in how to live as an overcomer each day as they grow in the knowledge of what the Blood has done for them. Kola's love and understanding for the Word of God makes this book a must read for all who want to grow in their understanding of the finished work of Christ on the Cross and apply those benefits into their lives gaining new insights and understanding of who they are in Him.

Greg J Daley
President, **International Fellowship of Ministries**

A fascinating incursion into the very heart of the matter: What does the blood referred to so often in our Scriptures mean as applied practically to our own lives? Is it more than the acknowledgement that Christ shed His blood for our sins? Pastor Kola courageously raises this important issue, bringing to each reader a new understanding and appreciation for a word often misused and misunderstood. Required reading for anyone who seeks to fully understand this concept."

Scott Volyn,
B.A., M.A., J.D., M.Div.
(Candidate)

In his latest book, Kola Emiola reminds us of the importance the blood of Jesus has, and the power that it holds. In The Miracle Working Blood, Kola takes us through biblical principles regarding the power of the blood of Jesus; a power that is still available to us today. In addition, Kola also shares practical insight for walking in victory by being washed by the blood of Jesus in our daily lives. By reading declarations and testimonies, you will receive head and heart knowledge of the power the blood of Jesus holds.

Jason Himmelberger
Founder and Senior Pastor of the Revolution Church
Port Angeles, WA

They know about the doctrine of the Blood but are ignorant of the life that is in it.

- Kola O. Emiola-

Introduction

This is the unveiling of the 'Dynamics of the Life in the Blood' or simply put, 'The Miracle Working Blood'. The Church, as a body, is gradually drifting away from this truth about 'Life' or has reduced the life in the Blood to a mere tradition. In turn this tradition has rendered the life ineffective.

Most of our 21st century Christian lyrics say little or nothing about the Blood. Many even consider the Blood as old fashioned and hence have removed it from their hymn books and translations. Some are not too sure there is actually life in the Blood. Some have even committed the Blood to the past. Praise God for the few that are taking advantage of the life in the Blood to change their lives and the lives of others. You too can be part of these few. You are in for an unforgettable journey to the power of God in the now and in the ages to come.

Many have termed the Blood an old fashioned phenomenon. I keep on wondering what is old about the Blood that cleanses sin and sets free from the bondage of sickness and establishes our glorious financial destiny in Christ. The Blood that has delivered us is delivering us and shall deliver us at last. The reality is that man is yet to fully experience the life that is in the Blood.

I do not agree with the doctrine of this modern day Christianity that has a form of love for the word but hates perfectly the Blood. I don't really agree with this modern day doctrine that divorces the Word from the Blood. At best, the modern day belief has only succeeded in giving mental knowledge without the power that accompanies the gospel. May be this situation can best be described in the words of Benjamin Franklin:

"He was so learned that he could name a horse in nine languages, so ignorant that he bought a cow to ride on."

When you take away the Blood, you deny me of everything I have in and through the Blood. Oh, no wonder we have many believers with big heads but they are thin at heart. They know about the doctrine of the Blood but are ignorant of the life that is in it.

What makes man the image and likeness of God is hidden in the Blood, not in our physical look or make up. The Blood is the carrier of God's DNA that makes man His image and likeness.

Whoever sheds man's blood, By man his blood shall be shed; For in the image of God He made man.   GENESIS 9:6

Blood is not life but it carries life.

Chapter One

....

Blood itself is nothing but a carrier of the life of God.

- Kola O. Emiola -

Winning Blood

LIFE CARRYING BLOOD

THE DRAMA in the Garden of Eden reveals how God created **man** from the dust of the earth. At a stage when it looked like God had completed His work on man but, then, man could not move, talk, see, feel, taste and think. There was no life in this newly created man. God desires to create something that will be second to nothing but Himself, God's intention seems not feasible. To the amazement and wonder of all Angels, and the entire earth, God brings on board the only thing that is required to make man to be in His image and likeness - the spiritual life of God.

And God breathed life into man and he became a living soul that could co-create, tender the ground and rule on the earth for God. Blood alone will not do this but the life in the blood. Blood itself is nothing but a carrier of the life of God. The blood is the physical carrier of the life of God. Life is spiritual but the blood itself is physical. The life of every living thing is packaged in the blood. The life in the blood is the divine breath of God. Friend, the meeting point of God's divinity and humanity is in the blood.

And the LORD God formed man of the dust of the ground, and breathed into his nostrils the breath of life; and man became a living soul.
GENESIS 2:7KJV

The Blood of Jesus is never an historic fact but a present day lifesaving thing. The reality is that the blood has the potential to expel sin, break curses, destroy poverty and break hardship. Most people are not denying the life in the blood, they only ignore it. You cannot be canalized regarding issues concerning the blood.

They count the Blood common; they look at the Blood as an ordinary thing. They simply look down on what the Blood has done, is doing and will do. Some simply believe what the Blood has done in saving them from sin but refuse to believe it is their weapon to be free from the present day's evil. They denied that the Blood has power to protect or deliver. Jesus blood is God's price for the redemption of the human race.

Now listen, life itself is not visible because life is spiritual, but it must have a physical carrier, and this carrier is the man's blood. So, the point at which divinity and man meet is the blood.

> **Friend, the meeting point of God's divinity and humanity is in the blood.**

Jesus' Blood is God's price for the redemption of the human race.

TURNING THE BATTLE IN YOUR FAVOUR

> *And Pharaoh said, "Who is the Lord that I should obey His voice to let Israel go? I do not know the Lord, nor will I let Israel go.*   EXODUS 5:2

The Israelites' stubborn enemy will not let them go despite the nine terrible plaques that God visited Egypt with. Even God knows that Pharaoh would not let them go until the blood was applied. The blood was God's final blow that set the Israelites free from the pain and burden of slavery.

It takes the blood of animals to humiliate the stubborn King of Egypt. The battle is once again about to turn in your favour as you take advantage of the Blood of Jesus, the Lamb of God, by faith. If the blood of animals could make such a mighty deliverance; friend, how much more the Blood of the only begotten Son of God to deliver you from sin and all its effects: sickness and poverty.

Jesus' Blood is God's price for the redemption of the human race.

Watch out, Satan, we draw the Blood line by faith. The Blood will sure undo all the lies of the enemy. Every lying vanity will be humiliated before the Blood of the Lamb of God.

They that observe lying vanities forsake their own mercy.   JONAH 2:8

Every lying symptom that the enemy is using to humiliate you is about to be permanently humiliated as you take full advantage of the life that is hidden in the Blood.

Satan, watch out, I am coming with the

Blood against you. Friend, keep reading do not stop now.

Two Blood Types

Then Mary said to the angel, "How can this be, since I do not know a man?"

And the angel answered and said to her, "The Holy Spirit will come upon you, and the power of the Highest will over-shadow you; therefore, also, that Holy One who is to be born will be called the Son of God. Luke 1:34-35

When man sins his blood becomes corrupted by the enemy. Death reigns in the human blood.

Therefore, just as through one man sin entered the world, and death through sin. (Romans 5:12)

Hear me; death is a result of sin. Sickness, disease, curse, lack, hardship are phenomena implying death manifesting in different forms. The Blood of Jesus removes sin and its effects because it is sinless Blood. God's life reigns in the Blood of Jesus. The Blood that flows in Jesus is divine. Mary provided the womb; the Holy Spirit overshadowed her to create way for the life of God to enter into her. The ever winning life of God was packaged in the Blood that flows in Jesus. This life is the only cure for the dying man. It is the eternal life of God.

What makes man the image of God is in the blood and not in the physical look or make up. The Blood is the carrier of God's DNA that makes man in the image and likeness of God. And this empowers man to carry out his assignment on earth: dominate, replenish and fruitful.

No man can dominate without a strong positive faith in the Blood. The Blood of Jesus announces to man that reigning again is possible. A man that is born again by the washing of the Blood can reign again if the Blood benefits are taken advantage of. It is a matter of being born again to reign again. The Blood is our principal instrument to dominate, rule and reign. As long as you look at the Blood as a historical fact and not a present day truth you remain a victim of your defeated enemy. Satan retains his control over your life and destiny by your own making.

Every man carries the DNA of his father in his blood. Jesus also carries the DNA of His Father, God, in His Blood. Jesus' Blood is different from man's blood because it carries the life of God.

EVERYONE, EXCEPT JESUS

And He has made from one blood every nation of men to dwell on all the face of the earth, and has determined their pre appointed times and the boundaries of their dwellings. ACTS 17:26

When Adam ate the forbidden fruit, His blood became poisoned by sin and all the effects of sin gained control of man. Man began to die from that day forward. Men suffer to live in liberty from poverty, sickness, failure and curses, except one man. Except Jesus. Every man, because of his descent from Adam, has, in his blood, sin, sickness and poverty. Only Jesus' Blood is exempted.

Jesus is the only exception because He was not born of the blood of Adam. He had the sinful flesh of man provided by His mother, but has the sinless Blood of His Father, God. It has been medically proven that from the moment of conception to the time of birth not one single drop of blood ever passes from the mother to the child. The mother contributes no blood at all. The blood is not conveyed by the mother but rather it is conveyed by the seed of the father. Jesus carries the Blood of

His Father.

The Blood that flows in the veins of Jesus is the Blood supplied only by God. Jesus Blood is never contaminated by sin, sickness or disease. It is not corrupted by any things here on earth that is why the life in this Blood can deliver man from all form of evil. You mean including this sickness? Yes, I mean EVERY effect of sin and any known and unnamed sickness.

The life in the Blood is God's ability made available to man by the Father to walk out of every prison. Yes, every prison.

First Exodus, Second Exodus

Now the blood shall be a sign for you on the houses where you are. And when I see the blood, I will pass over you; and the plague shall not be on you to destroy you when I strike the land of Egypt.   EXODUS 12:13

At the very time the Jews were celebrating the first exodus; Jesus was making atonement for the second exodus. The first exodus was not without the blood of animals, so also the second exodus is through the way of the Blood of Jesus, the Lamb of God. Freedom that will last is established always because of the blood. Our emancipation from the bondage of the devil was perfect and completely paid for by the Blood.

The blood of animals on the doorpost ended the oppression of the Israelites and gave way to their exit from the bondage of Egypt. This exit was physical. The Blood of the Lamb of God shed on the cross put an end to the reign and rule of Satan over man. The Blood of Jesus initiates and gives man the second exit from sin, sickness, and poverty.

Wow! Praise God. Every man in prison today is a prisoner by his own choice; the Blood of Jesus has opened the prison door. We can ALL now walk in freedom.

Turn you to the strong hold, ye prisoners of hope: even today do I declare that I will render double unto thee;
ZECHARIAH 9:12

The value you place on the Blood of Jesus will soon be revealed by your words. All that man lost in the garden were restored to him when Jesus shed His Blood on the cross. By that action, man was again restored to his original ruling state.

Friend, remember Jesus did not just shed His Blood so that he can bring man some self-help techniques but for man to be fully recreated and restored fully back to his original state: to rule and reign. Everywhere the life in the Blood is released by faith, the power of the enemy is completely broken. Every believer can enjoy Eden now if he or she so desires.

Every man in prison today is a prisoner by his own choice

The life of the new creation is in the Blood. No man can be recreated in the absence of the life that is in the Blood of Jesus.

Therefore, if anyone is in Christ, he is a new creation; old things have passed away; behold, all things have become new. 2 CORINTHIANS 5:17

POWERFUL ON EARTH, HONOUR IN HEAVEN

And they sang a new song, saying: "You are worthy to take the scroll, And to open its seals; For You were slain, And have redeemed us to God by Your blood Out of every tribe and tongue and people and nation, And have made us kings and priests to our God; And we shall reign on the earth. "Then I looked, and I heard the voice of many angels around the throne, the living creatures, and the elders; and the number of them was ten thousand times ten thousand, and thousands of thousands, saying with a loud voice:" Worthy is the Lamb who was slain To receive power and riches and wisdom, And strength and honor and glory and blessing!" And every creature which is in heaven and on the earth and under the earth and such as are in the sea, and all that are in them, I heard saying: "Blessing and honor and glory and power Be to Him who sits on the throne, And to the Lamb, forever and ever!" Then the four living creatures said, "Amen!" And the twenty- four elders fell down and worshiped Him who lives forever and ever. REVELATION 5:9-14

The cross of Christ, with what it has revealed about obedience to God, atonement for sin and the crushing defeat of the foes of divine authority, shows us a representative Man overcoming for mankind and preparing, through His own incumbency, a throne and a heavenly ministry for those who overcome through Him.

The Blood of Jesus is full of power and all of heaven honours the Blood of the first begotten son of God. The Blood becomes honoured in heaven because of what it has done on earth before the foundation of the earth. The man who does not honour the Blood cannot apply it by faith. The Blood you do not honour, the life it carries cannot respond to you. Honour the Blood and it will respond to you.

ALL BLOOD SPEAKS

And he said, What hast thou done? the voice of thy brother's blood crieth unto me from the ground. Genesis 4:10

to Jesus the Mediator of the new covenant, and to the blood of sprinkling that speaks better things than that of Abel. Hebrews 12:24

The life in the blood does not stop speaking even after death. Every blood says something, but what they speak differ. Abel's blood cried vengeance, Jesus' Blood cries mercy. Jesus' Blood cried penalty paid for. Abel blood cried cursed, Jesus' Blood says curse is done with and blessing has taken over. Jesus' Blood declares death is defeated and the life of God reigns hence forth.

All other voice becomes feeble when the Blood of Jesus speaks. And Jesus' Blood says we are entitled to all of the promises of God. That Blood speaks of who we are and what we have. It speaks to us of righteousness. It cries the sin problem is over eternally and effects of sin are done with.

The Blood of Jesus is constantly speaking the Word of God. But what are we saying? Are we speaking the Word, or are we saying things like:

What am I going to do?

I don't know how I am going to make it.

The doctors say there isn't any cure for this disease, or

The economy is too harsh against me

When we speak what God says in His word, we are agreeing with what the Blood says. Our agreement establishes our victory all times.

When Jesus said, "It is finished," He was announcing to the world that the supreme sacrifice had been paid. Satan's hold was finished. Satan has eternally defeated. Victory over Satan is now made possible.

SOMETHING ABOUT THE BLOOD

Now the promises and blessings of God are available to anyone who comes through the Blood of the Lord Jesus Christ.

God's Gift Wrapped

For the life of the flesh is in the blood, and I have given it to you upon the altar to make atonement for your souls; for it is the blood that makes atonement for the soul.'   LEVITICUS 17:11

The Blood has always been God's gift to man. It is a gift with purpose attached. It is for atonement. It is for purging of man's spirit, soul and body. We were reconciled back because Jesus shed His Blood. Every contamination was removed by the Blood. You are Blood washed. You are Blood wrapped. You are power clothed.

Every manifestation of grace is a gift from God. If it is given then it is a gift. It must be received by faith to enjoy the benefits of the gift. Eternal life is God's gift to man but this gift needs a carrier and therefore He decided to package it in the Blood of His only begotten Son.

The gift is concealed in the Blood. Life is hidden in the Blood. When God gave Jesus, He gave His Blood as well. Both the flesh and the Blood of Jesus were given the same time. You do not have to work for a gift. God expects us to receive the life packaged in His gift to the fullest.

Friend, you either receive a gift or you reject it. The choice is yours. How you receive a gift tells more about the value you put on the gift as well as the trust you have in the giver.

The above scripture clearly makes it plain that this life carrying Blood has been given to man for the saving and deliverance of his soul. No man works for this.

You are Blood washed. You are Blood wrapped. You are power clothed.

God gives it as a gift to ALL.

For God so loved the world that He gave His only begotten Son, that whosever believes in Him should not perish but have everlasting life.   JOHN 3:16

When God gave Jesus He gave His Blood as well. You cannot give the flesh without the blood. The life of the flesh is wrapped in the blood. God gave all of Jesus to man. His flesh and Blood were given at the same time. Both flesh and Blood must be received by faith. We have done nothing to deserve it. God gave it all. God did it all. Every time the Blood is received by faith it is always accompanied with freedom.

This life is not paid for nor worked for; we simply received it as a gift from God to us. Listen; because it is a gift many regard the Blood as something "common". To call it common implies that the Blood is inferior in quality; not different from others in ranking, to see nothing exceptional in or about the Blood. When you look down on the Blood of Jesus or you call it common, you are insulting the Spirit of grace. You treat the Blood common when you are limiting what God can do through the receiving of the Blood by faith.

So what do you think should be done to those who do not respect the Son of God, who look at the blood of the agreement that made them holy as no different from others' blood, who insult the Spirit of God's grace? Surely they should have a much worse punishment. HEBREWS 10:29 NCV

Chapter Two

The Blood of Jesus was not shed just to take us to heaven but to bring heaven down to the earth through His Church.

- Kola O. Emiola -

The Blood at Work

THE BLOOD, OUR SIN

and the blood of Jesus Christ His Son

MAN DID NOT KNOW SLAVERY, poverty or sickness until he ate from the forbidden tree. At the beginning man did not know fear or bondage in any form. Man mastered everything at creation until he sinned. Sin reduced man to become slave to everything.

What a drama indeed. From that point man sought a way out but God had a better way out. The only answer God has for sin is only in His Son's death. The power that destroys sin is hidden in this sin destroying Blood. No man can be freed from sin without passing through the exit of the Blood. You cannot enter into a covenant relationship with God without total acceptance of the Blood sacrifice of His only begotten Son. Adam ate the forbidden fruit by decision.

For the Blood to work, man must accept and apply it by his own decision. Jesus shed His Blood consciously as a sacrifice for our sin.

Friend, when Adam ate the forbidden fruit sin gained power and force to take away from man his identity, peace, prosperity and even health. What sin took away Jesus came to restore to man. This He did by paying the highest price with His Blood. That man would be messed up did not surprise God but Jesus still went ahead to die so that the mess would turn to message.

At the application of the Blood by faith prison doors were opened. Now, every slave can walk out free through the Blood. There is no alternative route to come out of the prison of sin to righteousness other than the Blood gate. The door sin opened, Jesus' Blood closed. Man, through Adam, sold himself to Satan through disobedience. From then man was daily paraded in the slave- market. Man served sin and became a slave to Satan.

Jesus went to the market place and paid the highest price with His Blood. The Blood was accepted by the Father. The Blood totally defeated Satan. The Blood cleanses man from sin and all that disfigured him. Through the Blood man is truly looked at as in the time past: the likeness and image of

God. The price for freedom was paid. The door to freedom was again open to man.

But friend, the only way out is the way of the Blood of Jesus. God will meet with a sinner but not without the Blood. Only the man cleansed by the Blood is indwelled by the Spirit. The Blood does not just cleanse, it keeps you clean always. The Blood cancels the debt and liability of sin

Through faith he kept the passover, and the sprinkling of blood, lest he that destroyed the firstborn should touch them. HEBREWS 11: 28

The Blood of Jesus settles the problem of sin forever. Only the man that calls the Blood "common" that sin still rules over. Power to live above sin is made available in the Blood and released by man's faith in the Blood The blood of bulls and goats only covered sin.

Only the Blood of Jesus took away sin totally and completely eternally. If the Blood can't stain you, then heaven will not receive you. Until you are washed in the Blood, you are doomed to be wasted. The sacrifice of the Blood of Jesus settled the problem of sin once and forever.

Here is how Hebrews 10: 14 put it:

For by one offering He has perfected forever those who are being sanctified.

Every cleansed sinner will appreciate the cleansing power in the Blood of Jesus. If there still remains a man in sin the Blood is the only thing that can deliver and cleanse from the yoke of sin.

To Him who loved us and washed us from our sins in His own blood
REVELATION 1: 5

THE BLOOD, OUR REDEMPTION

In Him we have redemption through His blood, the forgiveness of sins, according to the riches of His grace.
EPHESIANS 1:7

Our redemption is a total and complete removal from the reign of Satan into the Kingdom of Light. This redemption by the Blood of Jesus is a permanent deal. His death and resurrection was not just to visit man to comfort him in his state of slavery, sickness and poverty. Jesus did not come to earth to inspect man's situation. No, His paramount purpose was to buy us back from the slave market of Satan and never to return there anymore. The Blood of Jesus closed the door of slavery and opened to us a new way of living: FREEDOM AND DOMINION guaranteed.

Friends, the price of this freedom is much. Yes, I know we got it free by grace through faith. But on the contrary, Jesus did not secure our redemption free of charge. He paid the highest price to buy us back from Satan dominated market in His precious Blood. The price is the Blood of Jesus. The Blood of Jesus is God's price for man's redemption.

The eternal life of God flows through every drop of the Blood of Jesus. Satan's control over our lives, our bodies, our marriages, our jobs or businesses and our finances, is eternally broken and destroyed by the Blood paid for our redemption. The Blood secured our permanent freedom from Satan's control and reign. YOU ARE FREE NOW by THE BLOOD in Jesus' name

> *knowing that you were not redeemed with corruptible things, like silver or gold, from your aimless conduct received by tradition from your fathers, but with the precious blood of Christ, as of a lamb without blemish and without spot.* 1 PETER 1:18-19

Our redemption is eternal; Satan is similarly eternally defeated. The saints are eternally free. Now rise and see the chain of sin, sickness, poverty, failure fall off your neck in Jesus' Name through the Blood. It is time in your life to publicly display Satan's defeat. As we celebrate Jesus' victory through our freedom. Our redemption is ETERNAL. The Blood breaks EVERY chain.

Jesus did not come to earth to inspect man's situation. No, His paramount purpose was to buy us back from the slave market of Satan and never to return there anymore.

Not with the blood of goats and calves, but with His own blood He entered the Most Holy Place once for all, having obtained eternal redemption.
HEBREWS 9:12

The blood sets you free from the ownership of Satan. No longer an enemy of God but by the Blood, we become sons of God and joint heirs with Jesus Christ forever. Friends, because of Jesus' redemptive work, we are seated with Christ. Then take a positive step today; rise up to take the place secured for you by the Blood. It is the beginning of the devil fleeing from you. It is through this process man can enjoy Eden again on earth by the Blood.

and raised us up together, and made us sit together in the heavenly places in Christ Jesus EPHESIANS 2:6

Friend, I am thinking how far is this heavenly place that we shall be seated with Christ is from God's throne; whether it is close enough for Him to visit in the cool of the day like He did in the Garden of Eden but far that the devil can come close again.

far above all principality and power and might and dominion, and every name that is named, not only in this age but also in that which is to come. EPHESIANS 1:21

The Blood of Jesus was not shed just to take us to heaven but to bring heaven down to the earth through His Church. The Blood gives us complete and total salvation NOW.

And they sang a new song, saying: "You are worthy to take the scroll, And to open its seals; For You were slain, And have redeemed us to God by Your blood Out of every tribe and tongue and

*people and nation, And have made us
kings and priests to our God; And we
shall reign on the earth.*
REVELATION 5:9-10

THE BLOOD, YOUR PAST

*And according to the law almost all
things are purified with blood, and
without shedding of blood there is no
remission.* HEBREWS 9:22

The Blood of Jesus does not just take care
of our sin; it also purges all things not of
God in our lives including our past mistakes,
guilt that accompanied our mistakes and
pain of the past.

Friend, the Blood does not just clean our
past, it delivers us from the pain of the past
and protects from every attack either from
our past or an attack against our future.
Until a man is free from the heavy load of
guilt from his past mistakes it is difficult to
find joy in the present and strength to seize
the future. The burden will keep blocking
your ability to be the man you were created
to be.

The Blood of Jesus washes away our past
and the Name of Jesus opens up our future. It
is not important how much you had stained

your past, the Blood of Jesus will wash it as if it never existed. Hear me, only the Blood can break you away from the pain of the past. Many are held bound by the pain of the past that they cannot move into their future. Yes some are pressed down with the weight of the pain of the past that they cannot rise up and be counted for God.

Friend, whether you are chained or pressed down by the pain of your past, I announce to you today that the BLOOD of Jesus is enough to break every chain. Release your past to Jesus now and let His Blood wash it away. You are the only one who can hold on to your past. Your past cannot hold on to you when confronted with the Blood. The chain of the past becomes weak in the presence of the life carrying Blood. Let the Blood deliver you to a life of complete victory.

Listen, your mistakes cannot be forgotten with time. It can only be wiped away by the Blood of Jesus. Time does not heal, only the Word heals. Time does not take away pain, only the Blood does. Many run around daily in fear because of their past. You do not need to daily run away from your past, just confront it with the Blood of Jesus.

Friend, it is fruitless to reflect on your past, your fears and doubts without the

Blood. No self-help skills will wipe away the pain of your past, only the Blood of Jesus CAN. The Blood is ENOUGH to break every chain. I can see everything in your past that held you fast giving way NOW because the Blood has been applied.

Friend, God looks beyond your fault to meet your need because of the Blood. It is time you think about the Blood, talk about it, and sing about it until your faith in the Blood increases. You are not to come and apply the Blood once a year but all the time.

Friend, if you have been bornagain and washed in the Blood, your past has been cleansed. With God your past does not exist.

Brethren, I count not myself to have apprehended: but this one thing I do, forgetting those things which are behind, and reaching forth unto those things which are before,
PHILIPPIANS 3:13

Satan's control over our lives, our bodies, our marriage, our jobs or business and our finance is eternally broken by the Blood paid for our redemption. The Blood secured our permanent freedom from Satan's control and reign.

Blood covenant is saying I will give you my life, you have my love and protection forever till death do us part. Stop telling yourself how bad your past was; embrace perfection as revealed through the Blood. He paid it all for your sake.

The redemption only comes through the Blood of Jesus. Jesus did not shed His blood by accident but by eternal arrangement of God. Jesus, in redemption, paid man's penalty in His Blood and conquered Satan in the same. The work of Jesus on the cross is greater than any mistake you can ever make.

Friend, any man that allows his past to torment his today is calling the Blood of Jesus nothing. Your past is past because of what the Blood has done. Your present is a gift from God to enjoy because He lives.

The Blood, My Faith

Likewise He also took the cup after supper, saying, "This cup is the new covenant in My blood, which is shed for you. Luke 22:20

through whom also we have access by faith into this grace in which we stand, and rejoice in hope of the glory of God. Romans 5:2

When what you know about the Blood is not accurate, what you believe will be wrong. When what you expect to benefit from the Blood is small, it will show in what faith can do for you through the Blood. Faith is not expected to take full advantage of the Blood at that stage.

Everything about our faith is connected to the Blood. To underestimate the power in the Blood will be an overwhelming defeat to our faith. Covenant is what put doubt completely in silence. Where covenant is misunderstood or is not understood, faith cannot thrive.

The Mediator's Death Necessary For where there is a testament, there must also of necessity be the death of the testator. HEBREWS 9:16

Faith comes from hearing God's Word ROM. 10:17

If we don't hear that Jesus came to bring us back into intimate relationship with God, then we won't have faith for that and we won't experience it. If you do not hear about the truth of how Jesus paid for your healing fully, you won't believe that healing belongs to you. Whatever you do not hear you cannot believe.

Your faith becomes weak without the Blood. Faith works because covenant exists. Without the blood there is no covenant. The only covenant that God honoured and is committed to is the Blood covenant. Faith comes by hearing and hearing by the word of God. You will need to hear the word concerning the Blood.

Until the Blood is properly appreciated, you cannot take advantage of all that He made available to us by faith. Faith becomes important in the Blood of Jesus who is the author and finisher of our faith.

When what you know about the Blood is not accurate, what you believe will be wrong.

When we lightly esteem the Blood our faith becomes weak in battle, weak to win and walk in victory that is made accessible by His death and resurrection.

And Moses took half the blood and put it in basins and half the blood he sprinkled on the altar. Then he took the Book of the Covenant and read in the hearing of the people. And they said, "All that the Lord has said we will do, and be obedient." And Moses took the blood, sprinkled it on the people, and said, "This is the blood of the covenant which the Lord has made with you according to all these words.

Exodus 24:6-8

The blood and the book of covenant establish man in purpose and destiny. One cannot exist without the other. Until there is accurate hearing of what our covenant is all about no one develops faith in the Blood. Faith comes by hearing. No man honours the book without honouring the blood.

You cannot have faith in the book without having faith in the blood. You cannot separate the word from the blood. They are inseparable twins. The blood must be applied by faith. When we know what the word says about the blood, then faith begins.

The blood is the proof that God is committed to whatever He has promised in the book of covenant. We must have faith in the bread which is the body of Jesus and in the wine which is the Blood of Jesus. Pleading the Blood with disobedience to the word produces no faith.

Men are not always true to their words. The blood is the token that God will do what the covenant promises. Hallelujah! The power of God is wrapped in the blood and is made effective as we apply our faith in the blood.

Friend, faith in the blood is when you accept in totality all that the blood has done for you and entered into perpetually. Honouring the Blood makes you appreciate all that are yours by the Blood covenant. Covenant people are supernaturally positioned for power, protection and provision.

The blood is the token that God will do what the covenant promises.

Covenant people are blessed saints. Our faith will be ineffective to produce results until the blood is mixed with the word. It takes both the word and the blood to overcome the works of the evil one.

And they overcame him by the blood of the Lamb and by the word of their testimony, and they did not love their lives to the death. REVELATION 12:11

THE BLOOD, OUR PRAYER

Beloved, if our heart does not condemn us, we have confidence toward God. And whatever we ask we receive from Him, because we keep His commandments and do those things that are pleasing in His sight.

1 JOHN 3:21-22

No man can pray effectively when he lightly esteems the Blood that grants access to the Father. We come to the throne of grace through the Blood. We ask the Father in His name. Sin blocks the way to the Father, the road blocks were removed at the appearance of the Blood. The sin- problem was finally settled once for all. Now we can go in to receive all that the Blood made available to us NOW.

There is power in the name of Jesus only by His shed Blood and offered to the Father once and for all. Where there is no sin, there is no need for sacrifice again. The Blood of Jesus settled sin and its effects once and for all.

Now where there is remission of these, there is no longer an offering for sin.

Hold Fast Your Confession Therefore, brethren, having boldness to enter the Holiest by the blood of Jesus,
HEBREWS 10:18-19

We can all come into His presence without any shame or inferiority complex through the Blood gate: the blood of Jesus. The Father cannot deny you access when He sees you through the Blood of Jesus.

Friend, Jesus knew that the Father will not recognise you or your name. Try to cast a demon in any other name; you will surely invite more doing that. Jesus, by shedding His Blood, was given a name above all names and He gave that same name to you so that when you stand praying in that name is as if Jesus himself is praying. If the Father will not deny Jesus, He won't deny you whatever you ask the Father in His name. This is the secret of answered prayers.

And in that day you will ask Me nothing. Most assuredly, I say to you, whatever you ask the Father in My name He will give you. Until now you have asked nothing in My name. Ask, and you will receive, that your joy may be full.
JOHN 16:23-24

Take the Blood Now.

THE BLOOD, THE WORD

*And there are three that bear witness
on earth: the Spirit, the water, and the
blood; and these three agree as one.*
                                    I JOHN 5:8

The word without the Blood is ineffective.
Why? The life of the word is in the Blood. It
is the life in the Blood that makes the word
productive. Jesus is the word of God, the life
of Jesus is in the Blood. Without the Blood
there is no life in the Word. Whatever Jesus
is, the Blood is. Whatever Jesus does, the
Blood does.

Honouring the word without honour for
the Blood will result in a lifeless religion;
that is never a threat to the devil at all. Any
assembly where the word of God and the
Blood are honoured the manifestation of
the Spirit is always the bye product. When
this happens it produces all manner of the
deliverance from all the works of the devil.

*It is the Spirit who gives life; the flesh
profits nothing. The words that I speak
to you are spirit, and they are life.*
                                    JOHN 6:63

Every word of God has the Blood on it. The
word is Blood wrapped. The word of God

Honouring the word without honour for the Blood will result in a lifeless religion; that is never a threat to the devil at all.

spoken out of your mouth is the voice of the Blood covenant. Friend, if you know and understand that the Blood of Jesus is what makes God's word "yea and amen" then we can rise in active faith to believe and speak the promises of God loud and clear until every burden is lifted and yokes are destroyed.

Listen, the word came first, then the Blood that carries the life flows through. The two can never be separated from each other. Every flesh needs blood to carry out its function. The power or the life the flesh needs to function is hidden in the blood of the flesh.

And the Word became flesh and dwelt among us, and we beheld His glory, the glory as of the only begotten of the Father, full of grace and truth.
JOHN 1:14

There is no life in the book until it is sprinkled with the blood. Every believer who ignores the Blood also rejects the revelation.

He may know the letter but void of the revelation that makes for outstanding. The access to the mystery in the book is through the Blood. The word becomes difficult to obey without the strength that is supplied only by the Blood. God made provision for life through the Blood.

The word tells you what to do; the life in the Blood empowers you to do it. The word gives you the direction; the life in the Blood empowers you to go that direction. It is the life in the blood that gives power to obey the word, without the life in the Blood the word is of no benefit. When a believer believes the word, and sprinkles the Blood in the Name of Jesus no demon in hell can stand it because tremendous power is made available.

Though one may be overpowered by another, two can withstand him. And a threefold cord is not quickly broken.
ECCLESIASTES 4:12

The only thing in the world that pushes a man towards his destiny and brings him to fulfillment is nothing but the Word of God.

THE BLOOD, THE NAME

And being found in appearance as a man,, He humbled Himself and became

obedient to the point of death, even the death of the cross. Therefore God also has highly exalted Him and given Him the name which is above every name, that at the name of Jesus every knee should bow, of those in heaven, and of those on earth, and of those under the earth, and that every tongue should confess that Jesus Christ is Lord, to the glory of God the Father.
PHILIPPIANS 2:8-11

Even the name of Jesus, as powerful and awesome as it is cannot work effectively without the Blood. Because He has to die, shed the Blood for Him to receive the name above all names.

Friend, the implication of Jesus receiving a name that is above all names is that you will not need to go to the Father in your own name in prayers. Why? It is because the Father does not know you; you without God, you cannot have any access to Him. But if, instead, Jesus takes your place and speaks for you or makes any demand on your behalf, there is a quick response.

And whatever you ask in My name, that I will do, that the Father may be glorified in the Son. If you ask anything in My name, I will do it. JOHN 14:13-14

There is power in the name of Jesus only because He shed His Blood and offered it to His Father as a living sacrifice. The name of Jesus works today because the Blood is still speaking. Jesus becomes a name above all names through the way of the Blood. The name wins because the Blood won. Jesus' name is above all names. His Blood is above all blood. All other blood fails at the appearance of the Blood of Jesus.

The name and the Blood are inseparable because the life is in the Blood. Power and authority in the name only become operatives as we honour the Blood by faith and obedience. What we bind on earth is bound in heaven. The full power of heaven itself is released at the mention of His precious Name because of the precious Blood. We are not saved by Church membership; we are saved by the shed Blood of Jesus

Hear me, the Blood of Jesus carries all the power, spirit and that is residence in Jesus. There is no victory without battle. To be given the name above all other names He must first stain His robe in His own Blood.

He was clothed with a robe dipped in blood, and His name is called The Word of God. REVELATION 19:13

And the Egyptians were urgent upon the people, that they might send them out of the land in haste; for they said, We be all dead men.
EXODUS 12:33 KJV

And almost all things are by the law purged with blood; and without shedding of blood is no remission.
HEBREWS 9:22 KJV

THE BLOOD, THE ENEMY (DEVIL)

For I will pass through the land of Egypt on that night, and will strike all the firstborn in the land of Egypt, both man and beast; and against all the gods of Egypt I will execute judgment: I am the Lord.
EXODUS 12:12

The blood is the last instrument God used to break the will of Pharaoh over the Israelites. All the gods of Egypt suffered at the appearance of the blood of animal. Every wickedness of Satan and his demons is greatly punished at the appearance of the Blood of the only begotten Son of God. If the blood of animal can break the yoke of Egypt, the Blood of Jesus will certainly destroy the yoke of wickedness around any man's neck.

Your enemy's assignment in your life will fail at the appearance of the Blood. No devil can stand at the mention of the Blood of Jesus by faith. The life of God in the Blood is stronger than every form of death. The defeat of Satan on the cross was a classic one. He was defeated in three realms of the spirit, soul and body.

The victory of Jesus was an overwhelming victory it is established in spirit, soul and body. Say it boldly: Satan, by the Blood you are defeated eternally. I have victory in my spirit, soul and body. It is through the vehicle of the Blood that we enjoy our victory in Christ. We now reign in life because of the shed Blood. When the Blood was sprinkled the believer's dominion over the devil and his works was eternally settled and established. Now in Christ, he reigns over all in heaven, in the earth and under the earth.

It is like taking any drug, the doctor's prescription must be followed strictly in order to see the desired result. God gave us all the prescription to take advantage of the Blood. Firstly, stay in the house, you cannot be outside and want to enjoy the children's bread. For you to share in the inheritance you must be part of the family either by birth or adoption.

In Christ both are made possible because of the shed Blood. Secondly, stay under the Blood; you must be Blood -covered to stay free from our common enemy. For the Israelites to come out from the house of bondage, the blood protected them, the blood delivered them and the blood purged them of their past.

The Blood is a reminder to the devil that he had already lost the battle. The covenant of the Blood entered into by faith made us one with God when enforcing our victory over the enemy in the battle of life. Satan's defeat is just sure; there is no dispute about it. Praise God, by the Blood we overpower the devil and his evil works.

And they shall take some of the blood and put it on the two doorposts and on the lintel of the houses where they eat it... Now the blood shall be a sign for you on the houses where you are. And when I see the blood, I will pass over you; and the plague shall not be on you to destroy you when I strike the land of Egypt.   EXODUS 12:7, 13

The Church overcame the devil by the Blood of the Lamb and the word of their testimony. Friend, Satan doesn't fear you, he is terrified by the Blood that was shed at Calvary. This Blood gives us power over death, hell and the grave. By the Blood we rule and reign over all that the enemy has taken by deception.

We were set free from fear, guilt, sickness, disease, poverty and so much more because the Blood has been shed and applied by faith. Now we recover all because the Blood has been applied. Nothing can stand against you when you know the authority under which you operate because of the Blood.

His Blood has given you the victory over every battle you face! God does not desire His army to be prisoner of war to anything or anyone. Our accuser before God is eternally defeated through the Blood. The Blood forever closes the door of opportunity on the devil.

Forasmuch then as the children are partakers of flesh and blood, he also himself likewise took part of the same; that through death he might destroy him that had the power of death, that is, the devil; HEBREWS 2.14

The Blood of Jesus is the power that destroys all the works of the enemy.

THE BLOOD, THE ANGELS

Bless the Lord, you His angels, Who excel in strength, who do His word, Heeding the voice of His word.
PSALMS 103:20

And they overcame him by the blood of the Lamb and by the word of their testimony, and they did not love their lives to the death REVELATION 12:11

The voice of the word of God is hidden in the Blood because the Blood is the carrier of the life of God. The voice in the word of God that angels will listen to is in the Blood.

As you confess the finished work of Christ on the cross, angels begin to heed the word. No angel will work without the Blood. The reason is simple: angels don't listen to your word; they listen to the word of God.

It is the word of God that you believe and confess that the angels act upon and not your word, not the good saying of the people, not the old saying; not what your town's people are saying; not what your profession says; not what philosophers say. Angels hearken only to the word of God and do the word of God.

Friend, under the Old Covenant, the saints did not have authority over the angels, therefore they had to wait on them for help. Today, angels wait on us because now we can use the name of Jesus, which is greater than angels, to dispatch them to do their work - carrying out God's word that is released through your mouth.

A voice said:

Loose the four angels which are bound...
And the four angels were loosed
REVELATION 9:14-15 KJV

You can readily see that angels are meant to be loosed. And who has the power to loose angels? Jesus said that we do. We have the keys of the kingdom!

Listen friend, angels hearken — they listen and act upon--the VOICE of God's Word. We know that the Bible is God's Word. But angels don't hearken just to God's Word, but they hearken to the voice of His Word. Many open their bibles besides their pillow believing that it keeps demons away from them. But they wonder why the devil still afflicts them during the night. Take your bible and place it next to your ear. Stop! Listen!

What do you hear? NOTHING! Why? Because the bible does not have a voice unless we give it a voice. You are responsible for giving a voice to the written word. Your voice is important to any of God's words that you will enjoy. The instrument that makes angels to act on God's word is your MOUTH.

In other words, angels act on God's Word that we speak out of our mouth. They listen to us speaking God's Word. And when we speak God's Word, angels rush to perform it in our lives. Angels work for you because you confess who God is to you and what He will do for you because of the Blood of Jesus that was shed.

THE BLOOD, THE CHANGING TIMES

And they shall take of the blood, and strike it on the two side posts and on the upper door post of the houses, wherein they shall eat it.
                                          EXODUS 12: 7 KJV

So Moses brought Israel from the Red sea, and they went out into the wilderness of Shur; and they went three days in the wilderness, and found no water.

And when they came to Marah, they could not drink of the waters of Marah, for they were bitter: therefore the name of it was called Marah.

EXODUS 15:22-23 KJV

Then Moses said:

Thus says the Lord:' About midnight I will go out into the midst of Egypt; and all the firstborn in the land of Egypt shall die, from the firstborn of Pharaoh who sits on his throne, even to the firstborn of the female servant who is behind the hand mill, and all the firstborn of the animals. Then there shall be a great cry throughout all the land of Egypt, such as was not like it before, nor shall be like it again. But against none of the children of Israel shall a dog move its tongue, against man or beast that you may know that the Lord does make a difference between the Egyptians and Israel.

EXODUS 11:4-7

Every child of God that attempts to survive in this time and season without the Blood will certainly partake of the confusion that befalls men. No sense dominated man will want the Blood, sing the Blood or take the Blood in a time like this when all nations are living in delusion: wars, rumours of wars, economic failures, terrorist attacks, diseases that were not known before, etc. This is truly the midnight hours.

Financial institutions seem to have lost control, protests are all over our streets, killing and war and rumours of wars in all nations.

Friend, this is not different from what the Israelites experienced in Egypt when they were under bondage until they came 'under the blood'. The Blood of Jesus will ensure that you enjoy divine exemption and supernatural deliverance from every evil that is common to men. The Blood will surely deliver you from all fears. It is finished.

All you will ever need in this uncertain time are made ready by the finished work of Christ on the cross. It has happened before, the blood of animal delivered them. It is happening now before us all, only the Blood of Jesus can deliver now and eternally.

It is time to take cover 'under the Blood of Jesus' now. No man under the cover of the Blood will certainly partake of the evil common to man. Satan and his agents suffer greatly when the blood is invoked. If the blood of animal could deliver from the terror of Pharaoh, how much more, the Blood of the son of God can deliver from all of hell and Satan himself. Times and season change but the Blood of Jesus is the same forever. It carries the same life of God in it all the time and in every season.

Jesus Christ is the same yesterday, today, and forever.
HEBREWS 13:8

Every life difficult situation submits at the presence of the Blood. There is no need in your future that is not provided for in the Blood.

Listen, you will never have a need that is too costly that the price Jesus paid with His Blood will not cover. The Blood has no respect for the devil's opinions. The life in the Blood always releases power to overcome every known or unknown resistance. No resistance in hell is stronger than the precious Blood of Jesus. In this season when no one has come to speak up for man, not even our politicians.

Know this: the Blood has and will always speak for you. The Blood speaks peace over all that pertains to you.

to Jesus the Mediator of the new covenant, and to the blood of sprinkling that speaks better things than that of Abel. HEBREWS 12:24

THE BLOOD, MY HOPE

Return to the stronghold, You prisoners of hope (tiqwâ). Even today I declare That I will restore double to you
ZECHARIAH 9:12

The only tangible proof and guarantee that we have our expectation and desire in life is still the same today as it was with Rahab. It is in the finished work of the Blood of Jesus. Without the Blood every situation becomes hopeless. All of our hope for the past, the present and the future is completely by faith in what the Blood of the only begotten Son of God has provided.

If Rahab and her family could not be delivered without the blood, friend, you have no escape route beside the Blood. If any man will have hope for the future it must be because of what the Blood has purchased and done for us all. Any victory in the future is because of the victory of Jesus over Satan when He shed His Blood. Any dominion in the days ahead will only exist because Jesus defeated Satan completely when the Blood was sprinkled.

unless, when we come into the land, you bind this line (tiqwâ)of scarlet cord in the window through which you let us down, and unless you bring your father, your mother, your brothers, and all your father's household to your own home.   JOSHUA 2:18

There is hope (tiqwâ) in your future, says the Lord, That your children shall come back to their own border.
                                        JEREMIAH 31:17

Hear me: there is hope for tomorrow beyond the failure of yesterday because of the Blood only. Hope is what makes people rejoice about the future. Life is worst without hope. The number of people committing suicide is on the rise because hope has become a scarce commodity today. No hope from our media. We have self -help seminars everywhere because of man's hopelessness. Only the "cord of the Blood" will give man a true hope.

Hope is the brightness within that makes you to face the darkness with confidence. Hope will give you strength and joy to keep going.

Now hope does not disappoint, because the love of God has been poured out in our hearts by the Holy Spirit who was given to us.   ROMANS 5:5

If you are too big to be stained by the Blood, you are too small to enjoy the benefits of the Blood.

Friend, only the man under the Blood has the assurance of his expectation being met. The Blood was not done with in the first Church. It is still the agent that carries the life of God to all generations. If you put the Blood on only 'yesterday' you will be a 'victim' of today. If the Blood is not for now your tomorrow is bleak and miserable. The Blood gives hope to all generations. It is an everlasting Blood. The Blood opens the door of hope to all

So this day shall be to you a memorial; and you shall keep it as a feast to the Lord throughout your generations. You shall keep it as a feast by an everlasting ordinance.
EXODUS 12:14

Everything that attempts to deem your hope for the future Jesus Blood will destroy

How God anointed Jesus of Nazareth with the Holy Ghost and with power: who went about doing good, and heal-

*ing all that were oppressed of the devil;
for God was with him.*   ACTS 10: 38

Everything that wants to disgrace you in
the future the Blood has already disgraced
NOW. There is no shame in your future
because of the finished work of Christ.
Every harsh situation the enemy and his
agents have planned against you will turn
in your favour.   Living without hope is
oppression. It is hard to wake up without
hope for the day or future. Hopeless people
are disconnected; disconnected from God,
disconnected from the family, disconnected
from fellowship, disconnected from every
relationship and disconnected from living.
The fear of the unknown weighs many down.
Hopelessness kills man's passion to pursue.
It kills initiatives, slows down and destroys
passion to live. A man without hope cannot
find meaning in the future -

*But for him who is joined to all the liv-
ing there is hope, for a living dog is better than a dead lion.*
                                ECCLESIASTES 9:4

To have hope is to have an expectation for
the future, a trust in attaining or becoming
that future, patience with tenacity while
awaiting it, the desirability of the associated
benefits and confidence in the divine

promises of God contained in the scripture

according to my earnest expectation and hope that in nothing I shall be ashamed, but with all boldness, as always, so now also Christ will be magnified in my body, whether by life or by death. PHILIPPIANS 1:20

THE BLOOD PROTECTION

and nothing shall by any...
LUKE 10:19

No weapon fashioned against you shall prosper... ISAIAH 54 : 17

For He shall give His angels charge over you, To keep you in all your ways
PSALMS 91:11

Absolute protection is always available for those who stay under the Blood always. Until the Blood is used by faith it lacks the effectiveness to protect. No demon in hell is strong enough to cross the Blood line.

The destroyer was made impotent by the Blood. We are washed in the Blood and clothed by the Blood. We are created to live by all that the Blood provided access to. We came out of slavery by the Blood and we stay in freedom only by the Blood. We are saved to stay under the covering of the Blood. What the word of God says is that 'If I see the blood' and not 'if I see your prayers', and not 'if I see your tithe'. Tithe without the Blood becomes ineffective. The word of God does not say 'if I see your good works'; works without the Blood returns man back to the law, not even if you are sanctified.

Now the blood shall be a sign for you on the houses where you are. And when I see the blood, I will pass over you; and the plague shall not be on you to destroy you when I strike the land of Egypt EXODUS 12:13

If the blood of animal delivered the Israelites from death the superior Blood of Jesus can do much more. The Blood of Jesus becomes the only 'sign' that can save from all evil. The word 'sign' means evidence, proof, miracle mark, the distinguishing mark. I do not know any other sign that is stronger than the Blood of Jesus. The Blood is the only thing that will set you apart from all that is coming against man today and the future.

Friend, when the destroying angel saw the blood on the doors he did not dare to enter; no, not even to challenge it. The devil cannot attempt coming near you when what he sees now is not the blood of animal on the doors but the true Blood of the Son of God on the lips of believers, the doors of the temple of God

Do you not know that you are the temple of God and that the Spirit of God dwells in you?
I Corinthians 3:16

Listen, if the Blood is constantly applied on the gate to your temple then here is your daily experience - upper hand over evil all the time. The devil cannot come near the gate sprinkled with the BloodProver- Proverbs 14:19The evil will bow before the good, And the wicked at the gates of the righteous.

Come on, friend; raise the red flag now in faith so that every evil will   submit at the raising of the Blood. You have complete refuge under the Blood of Calvary, where no power of the enemy can penetrate. You can declare before all of hell and death because the Blood has been applied.

No evil shall befall you, Nor shall any plague come near your dwelling;" yes what destroyed others cannot destroy you, you are Blood cover, you are protected by the life carrying Blood of Je-

sus - Hebrews 11:28"By faith he kept the Passover and the sprinkling of blood, lest he who destroyed the firstborn should touch them   PSALMS 91:10

THE BLOOD, DIVINE DIRECTION

Then he brought Aaron's sons. And Moses put some of the blood on the tips of their right ears, on the thumbs of their right hands, and on the big toes of their right feet. And Moses sprinkled the blood all around on the altar.
LEVITICUS 8:24

Friends, the Blood will clean and sanctify all that enters into a man's ear if what came into the ear of Aaron, the Priest, needed to be cleansed. What enters the ear of the contemporary business man, student, politician, wife, husband and children needs cleansing and sanctification most especially during these days of high tech that comes with all manner of polluted information.

You may not be able to stop all these information that damage the identity of men and rob them of all that are made available by the Blood but you can prevent them from finding way through you ear to your heart. No man who despises the Blood can claim to truly be led on the affairs of life.

Therefore take heed how you hear. For whoever has, to him more will be given; and whoever does not have, even what he seems to have will be taken from him   LUKE 8:18

It is a fact of life that a man's thoughts will be fed by what constantly comes through his ears. A man's life goes in the direction of his dominant thought. What you are constantly hearing will determine your understanding; you can only begin to obey as you constantly hear God's word. What you obey reveals either wisdom or foolishness on your part. If you believe in the Blood, it will keep Satan away from your thought life. What the Prophet Isaiah said in Isaiah 6:10 confirm this position:

And their ears heavy, This means to be inattentive and disobedient. It implies that one is dull in hearing. This is the ear that hears everything except what is provided for him through the finished work of Christ. He knows about all the trouble he is going through but knows little and hears close to nothing of the freedom that comes by the same Blood that saved him. He is saved from hell but lives like in hell.

Friend, a man with devil inspired thoughts is far from divine direction. Your thoughts in life must be strengthened in line with God's word to be led of the Lord especially with all the noise around us today capable of causing distraction.

It is wisdom to protect your ears with the Blood daily. Your ear is the path to wisdom and understanding.

making your ear attentive to wisdom and inclining your heart to understanding;   PROVERBS 2:2

You cannot have a Blood cleaned ear and still be willing to walk in disobedience. The life in the Blood will not speak contrary to God's will for your life.

Your ears shall hear a word behind you, saying, "This is the way, walk in it,   ISAIAH 30:21

Whether you turn to the right or to the left, one fact remains constant: all devils in hell cannot penetrate the Blood. You can see that men are overtaken and overpowered by all other information that does not have its root in the finished work of Christ. Even when men run helter-skelter to gather information but it makes him, his situation and the world grow worse.

Listen, no other time than now in the history of man, will you need to daily sprinkle the Blood upon your ears. If you must guard your mind then you cannot ignore what you allow to enter your mind through the gate of your ear.

It is wisdom to protect your ears with the Blood daily. Your ear is the path to wisdom and understanding.

A man's ear tests every word and this leads the man to the direction he will choose to go. No man enters into God's purpose for his life with his ear blocked or closed. Your ear is the receiver of the divine revelation.

Does not the ear test words as the palate tastes food? JOB 12:11

The Blood will keep Satan away from his thought life, his work life and wherever he shall set his foot upon.

Friend, like Aaron's ears and that of his children consecrated by the blood of animal, let your ears be consecrated or set apart to hear His leading by the Blood of Jesus to hear only God's voice and go His direction all your life. The days of confusion have come to an end in your life today in Jesus' name. You are set apart from the multitude in the valley of indecision because the Blood has been applied.

THE BLOOD, YOUR EARTH

Then to Adam He said, "Because you have heeded the voice of your wife, and have eaten from the tree of which I commanded you, saying, 'You shall not eat of it': "Cursed is the ground for your sake; In toil you shall eat of it All the days of your life. Both thorns and thistles it shall bring forth for you, And you shall eat the herb of the field. In the sweat of your face you shall eat bread Till you return to the ground, For out of it you were taken; For dust you are, And to dust you shall return
GENESIS 3:17-19

And He said, "What have you done? The voice of your brother's blood cries out to Me from the ground. So now you are cursed from the earth, which has opened its mouth to receive your brother's blood from your hand. When you till the ground, it shall no longer yield its strength to you. A fugitive and a vagabond you shall be on the earth.
GENESIS 4:10-12

When He opened the fifth seal, I saw under the altar the souls of those who had been slain for the word of God and for the testimony which they held. And they cried with a loud voice, saying, "How long, O Lord, holy and true, until You judge and avenge our blood on those who dwell on the earth?
REVELATION 6:9-10

Then, behold, the veil of the temple was torn in two from top to bottom; and the earth quaked, and the rocks were split, and the graves were opened; and many bodies of the saints who had fallen asleep were raised;
MATTHEW 27:51-52

So when the centurion and those with him, who were guarding Jesus, saw the earthquake and the things that had happened, they feared greatly, saying, "Truly this was the Son of God;
MATTHEW 27:54

I like how the Message version paraphrases this happening recorded in Matthew 27:54

The captain of the guard and those with him, when they saw the earthquake and everything else that was happening, were scared to death. They said, "This has to be the Son of God!

So when Jesus had received the sour wine, He said, "It is finished!" And bowing His head, He gave up His spirit. JOHN 19:30

Man's sin gave Satan legal access to the earth. It must come to notice that every time man sins from the time of Adam the earth also suffers the effect of man's sin

Cursed is the ground for your sake; In toil you shall eat of it all the days of your life GENESIS 3: 17

It is man's sin that gave Satan freedom to his reign and terrors on earth. What was lost in Adam, Jesus restored to man when He shed His Blood on the cross.

Jesus Blood says no to Satan's rule and reign. Every blood that is shed on earth has an effect on the ground it touches. It either blesses or curses. When Cain spilled his brother's blood, the earth became cursed as soon as the blood hit the ground.

Friend, hear me, man does not have the experiential knowledge of curse until Adam sinned. The first word that proceeded from the mouth of God to man was blessing. Consequent upon the blessing, man (Adam) became used to abundance. The blessing worked for him and nothing worked against him. That is the reason why man hates all that is associated with curse. Until sin came man knew only blessing. Sin makes man to have the experience of blessing and cursing

Then God blessed them, and God said to them, "Be fruitful and multiply; fill the earth and subdue it; have dominion over the fish of the sea, over the birds of the air, and over every living thing that moves on the earth. GENESIS 1:28

Every innocent blood shed in war cries for vengeance. But praise God, the effect of the Blood of Jesus was shed to enforce the will of God on earth. It is the means by which we overcome the accuser of the brethren. As long as men keep on shedding the blood of innocents all over our earth, we will keep hearing a cry for justice.

It only takes a coward to kill innocent babies. Any coward who supports abortion has the blood of babies on his hand. I speak boldly that this coward needs to be made clean by the Blood of Jesus. Abortion is simply punishing 'the innocent one within' for the mistake of two adults.

No one needs to be punished for your mistakes; Jesus was punished once and forever for your today's mistakes and those of anyone in the future. The Blood is stronger than ALL your MISTAKES. Your days on the earth are blessed courtesy of the blood.

And there are three that bear witness on earth: the Spirit, the water, and the blood; and these three agree as one.
1 JOHN 5:8

Because the creature itself also shall be delivered from the bondage of corruption into the glorious liberty of the children of God   ROMANS 8:21

When the blood of Abel touched the earth, it cried for justice and God cursed the earth but when the earth drank from the Blood of Jesus, Jesus' Blood cried to God for MERCY and God blessed the earth and pronounced PEACE on earth.

Jesus does not just get the devil out of heaven into the earth but he came into the enemy's territory and shed his Blood. The Blood that flowed at Calvary was not wasted:

it did not fall to the ground and disappear.

Friend, when the Blood of the only Son of God hits the ground, the doubly cursed ground was doubly blessed. Yes, I mean when the Blood hits the ground all sicknesses on earth were destroyed by the Blood from His back. All curses, including financial hardship, were destroyed by the Blood that flows from His hands and hit the ground. Again the land will work for man not against him. Come on, praise the Lord.

I like the life that is packaged in the Blood. It was not by power, when that life hit the ground the ground gave up; there was an earthquake. Now we can enjoy Eden here again. The blockages on your blessing have been removed by the Blood. Henceforth, His Blood begins to speak victory over the earth as it is in heaven. From the time Jesus Blood touches the earth, the will of heaven is made possible on earth because the ruler of this world became powerless as power was taken away from him to hurt again.

The first earthquake recorded in the New Testament was recorded at the crucifixion. The bible says when the centurion and all the soldiers guarding Jesus saw the earthquake and all the things that had happened, they marveled. All the things that made the earth a curse gave way as the life in the Blood destroyed their power over man and all that he does on earth. They saw the power of sin destroyed, the force of sickness frustrated, poverty surrendered as the Blood hit its foundation.

Oh, today I pray that your eyes will be opened so that you can see all that happened on the cross. There is no power the devil has again expect the one you give him through ignorance. That is why Jesus said: 'it is finished'. What that means is that there was nothing else more to do for you than to enjoy your royal inheritance. Now all things are possible.

THE BLOOD, THE BLESSING

Christ has redeemed us from the curse of the law, having become a curse for us (for it is written, "Cursed is everyone who hangs on a tree"), that the blessing of Abraham might come upon the Gentiles in Christ Jesus, that we might receive the promise of the Spirit through faith. GALATIANS 3:13-14

Jesus' sacrificial death does not only set us free from sin, but His death delivered us from living under the heavy load of curse now and forever. A curse is what makes a man to become aware of sins. Sin deformed the man created by God in His image. The Blood covenant, when activated, will move God to go to war and fight for you. The curse of the law includes sin, sickness and poverty. Jesus broke the curse and erased every effect of it in His Blood.

The shedding of Jesus' blood is how far the curse of poverty could go. Jesus already paid the price for our prosperity. No sickness can travel beyond the 39 stripes at His back. Every known and unknown blessing has been provided for through the Blood.

Come on, shout it; 'NO MORE CURSE'! When Jesus shed the Blood God paid FOR all you will ever need to enjoy God in this life.

Yes, declare it NOW by faith: 'THE BLOOD PAID IT ALL'!

The Blood of Jesus is what sealed our covenant with God and removed every doubt and reason for it. This covenant between us and God is for us to become one single entity with Him. Each one lives for each other. We live for God, but the truth is, God also lives for us.

What, God lives for me? Yes, God and you become indivisible covenant partners sealed by the Blood of Jesus. What concerns you becomes His concern. The blood covenant removes every doubt and settles every question. The Blood of Jesus is the only door through which a man can come into ALL the blessings of God. The power to enjoy all of God blessings now and eternity is hidden in the Blood.

Friend, to receive all of God's blessings nothing is required except faith in the Blood of Jesus.

My covenant I will not break, Nor alter the word that has gone out of My lips.
PSALMS 89:34

THE BLOOD, MY MIND

how much more shall the blood of Christ, who through the eternal Spirit offered Himself without spot to God, cleanse your conscience from dead works to serve the living God?
HEBREWS 9:14

"for it is the blood that makes atonement for the soul.
LEVITICUS 17: 11

If a man has any problem, the first thing a doctor calls for is the blood test. Any trouble in the blood, troubles the entire human system. Trouble in the blood is a trouble in the entire man.

Our blood is designed by God to fight in two ways: first to provide defence to the body against all kinds of external organisms or diseases. Secondly, our blood fights within (internally) by preventing any diseases from taking root on the inside. The Blood of Jesus is a weapon for both defence and offence. It will destroy every weapon thrown against you from outside. Every tongue raised against you shall utterly fail.

You shall be hidden from the scourge of the tongue, And you shall not be afraid of destruction when it comes.
JOB 5:21

Yes, for sure, it will silence every voice and noise of the enemy coming from within you. No judgment against you from the enemy will stand. The voice of condemnation will be silenced by the Blood. Life will prevail over death as you allow the Blood to purge your mind

There is therefore now no condemnation to those who are in Christ Jesus,

who do not walk according to the flesh,
but according to the Spirit.

ROMANS 8:1

From childhood man has been fed with
many junks. A new born baby knows no
fear until an adult teaches him especially his
mother. He gets into the school and there he
is fed with more negative thoughts. Coming
to the church he finds religion and his mind
are wrapped with all man's thoughts expect
the knowledge of the Living God. Evil
becomes natural to man created to enjoy all
of God's best. Listen, only the Blood can set
your mind free.

The mind can be cleansed to serve God.
There is the need for the mind to be set free
to dream God's dreams. The mind must be
liberated to enjoy freedom truly. The mind
needs freedom to lay hold of opportunities
provided by the Blood. Not only does the
blood bring us forgiveness from our sins, it
also cleanses us from sin.

The Blood helps cleanse us from the stain
of sin in our lives. It can purge our minds.
The Blood has a cleansing power. God
does not only forgive but also He, through
the Blood, cleanses you from the stain and
damage of sin. The Blood destroys the
destroying power of sin.

But if we walk in the light as He is in the light, we have fellowship with one another, and the blood of Jesus Christ His Son cleanses us from all sin.
1 JOHN 1:7

One of the ways to free your mind from double-mindedness is through constant confession of the Blood over your mind by faith. Sprinkle the door of your mind with the Blood in order to destroy the deception of the devil. When a man's mind is bound by negative thought and the Blood is sprinkled by faith, freedom is guaranteed. A free mind results in a free body. A weak mind is a weak body. Poor mind is the reason for poor pockets. Dull mind is the reason for dull lives.

let us draw near with a true heart in full assurance of faith, having our hearts sprinkled from an evil conscience and our bodies washed with pure water.
HEBREWS 10:22

Even though all of our minds have been corrupted by sin and seared as with a hot iron, (1 Timothy 4:2), Christ, through the Blood, can cleanse our consciences. We are able to live right lives and think right thoughts once again in Christ. This is great news for those who are burdened by a sinful past and corrupted conscience.

We are bought back from a life lived devoid of meaning and are brought into a relationship with God and the ability to live in His will and with purpose. That is to say, he presents the Blood as his only answer to the accusations of the enemy.

THE BLOOD, YOUR HEALING

who Himself bore our sins in His own body on the tree, that we, having died to sins, might live for righteousness — by whose stripes you were healed.
1 PETER 2:24

When the price of your healing is too high for science, Jesus paid the price in His Blood. Your healing is purchased by the precious Blood of Jesus. You are free to be healed. All that was lost in Adam, including HEALING, were restored in Christ through the vehicle of the Blood of Jesus.

Friend, if the Blood of Jesus is enough to take away sin, then it is more than enough to take away the effects of sin: sickness and poverty. Jesus, by whose stripes you were healed, deals with man's sickness before dealing with his sin. Friend, taking away sin was the final blow on the devil. If no man can be saved without the shedding of Blood, no man can be healed without the sprinkled Blood.

Man will never face a disease that the Blood cannot humiliate and destroy. This divine Blood of the Son of God will destroy whatever disease or sickness that is named; be it cancer, AIDS, Ebola. Our body was bought back from sickness and diseases with the Blood. He became Lord over sickness with His Blood.

Or do you not know that your body is the temple of the Holy Spirit who is in you, whom you have from God, and you are not your own? For you were bought at a price; therefore glorify God in your body and in your spirit, which are God's I CORINTHIANS 6:19-20

Go to communion with the expectation to be freed from every sickness and anything that does not make life EASY for you. By receiving communion, we are partaking of everything Jesus' sacrifice provided: salvation, peace, prosperity and HEALING. Every blood related disease and sickness suffer greatly at the appearance of the Blood of Jesus. Satan is the author of all that damages our body and skin. Your blood is cleansed of all that destroys now in Jesus name.

For I will cleanse their blood that I have not cleansed: for the Lord dwelleth in Zion. JOEL 3:21 KJV

The Blood, without your faith to release the life in it, will do your body no good. The life you have in the Blood defeats sickness and defeats disease eternally. You have to believe what the word says about the Blood to enjoy the benefit of healing through the Blood. Good lyrics about the Blood without your faith, release no power to heal you. Jesus came, was beaten, hanged, bled, died and rose all because of you. The Blood he shed now carries the life of God, won't receive this life into your body to stop the dying process initiated by Adam's sin and continues by sickness. All the benefits of the Blood is received by having active faith in the finished work of Christ.

The life in the Blood always responds to faith. Life is always attracted to faith. Fear attracts death.

Listen, your faith in the Blood is what cleanses you. It is your faith in the Blood that will also heal you. Blood is loaded with power but your faith will release it to work for you. Faith releases the power of God into action in your life. Whenever the Blood is applied, power is released. Faith in the Blood releases divine energy for healing.

And the Lord will take away from you all sickness, and will afflict you with none of the terrible diseases of Egypt which you have known, but will lay them on all those who hate you.

DEUTERONOMY 7:15

THE BLOOD, OUR CONFESSION.

And they overcame him by the blood of the Lamb and by the word of their testimony, and they did not love their lives to the death.

REVELATION 12:11

Every word of God has Blood in it. The word of God that comes out of your mouth is the voice of the blood covenant. If we know that the Blood of Jesus is what makes God's word 'yea and amen' then we can rise up in faith to believe and speak the promises of God loud till the yoke of the enemy is broken.

The life in the Blood of Jesus is made active and effective by your confession. The devil cannot resist the Blood when mixed with faith in our heart and declared through our mouth.

As you confess the Blood, it is applied in every situation by faith. You begin to take advantage of all that the Blood made available to you by speaking the Blood. That is the starting point; because all that your faith stands for in the Blood is confession. Faith involves believing and speaking. If you believe the Blood then speak the Blood.

The devil daily brings up against you all manner of accusation. Jesus has already defeated him for you once and for all when the Blood was shed on the cross. But to enforce that victory over the devil now on earth, your confession of the Blood and agreement with the word become the instrument that Jesus will make use of in His present day ministry.

Every time you call on the Blood the devil trembles, because that is a testimony of your victory. Come on, friend, stop now and shout the Blood of Jesus! Your confession does not only go to Jesus in heaven, it also defeats the devil and thirdly releases God's power on your behalf.

The light of God's word exposes the works of darkness. The life in the Blood destroys the works of darkness and when faith in the word meets with confession in the Blood, power is made available. The devil will surely flee as in terror. There is this old saying that you 'light a candle to curse the darkness'.

Satan is not afraid of you as a person but he fears the promises. The gospel is the message of all that the Blood has done that require a VOICE. The life in the shed blood of Jesus is made active and effective by our confession-The devil cannot resist the Blood when mixed with faith in our hearts and declared through our mouth. Speak your faith out loud concerning what the Blood of Jesus has accomplished for you, knowing that your breakthrough is very near and sure. The light of God's word exposes the works of darkness; the life in the Blood destroys the works of darkness when faith in the word meet with confession in the Blood, power is made available. The devil will surely flee as in terror.

Chapter Three

Blood itself is nothing but a carrier of the life of God.

- Kola O. Emiola -

The Five Blood Access To Power

FRIEND by now you should have known that the **Blood** was not just to wash away your sins but also grant you access to all that is your benefit as a son and daughter of the Most High. Every citizen of any kingdom has some benefits that are exclusively reserved for him or her. Our Kingdom is not different; every one washed by the Blood of the Son of God has benefits made available and accessible only by the Blood.

When Jesus was beaten, wounded, tormented, scourged, and nailed to the cross, Blood poured from His back, head, hands, and feet. He was also pierced in His side. Each part from which His Blood flowed is significant because it represents each aspect of our deliverance from the kingdom of darkness.

Here are some of the things the Blood has done for you. It is yours just for the receiving.

Bless the Lord, O my soul, And forget not all His benefits
PSALMS 103:2

It is time to let the Blood deliver to you all your benefits and set you free from all forms of blockades the enemy has put on your way. Please stay with me.

HIS HEAD

And the soldiers twisted a crown of thorns and put it on His head, and they put on Him a purple robe.
JOHN 19.2

Blessings are on the head of the righteous, But violence covers the mouth of the wicked PROVERB 10:6

Roman soldiers plaited a crown of thorns and pressed it on Jesus' head until Blood began to flow from the Son of God's head. A man's head controls the entire body. The head is the control centre of life. Whatever happens to a man's head will affect the rest of his body. The blood that flowed from His head served us permanently for our freedom from every curse.

When a curse lands on a man, it falls on the head first, and then it proceeds to affect the entire life of the man and all he does. Same with blessings, when blessing is placed upon a man it falls on his head first. Then the blessing affects all that he does. The man's head is the point of contact for blessing.

That is why in the Old Testament, a father placed hands on the children's head to provoke blessing upon them.

Friends, in the New Testament also, hands are placed on the head to bless and to bring healing power on the sick.

Simply put, a curse is an empowerment to fail, and there is a cause for every curse.

Like a flitting sparrow, like a flying swallow, So a curse without cause shall not alight.   PROVERBS 26:2

Thorns are a symbolic representation of a curse. When a man's life is all 'thorns', it is full of frustration, difficulties, obstacles, defeat, sickness, untimely death, poverty, sorrow and all forms of evil.

Listen, when Adam sinned, the ground was cursed with thorns and thistle because of Adam's disobedience. From that point until Christ, hardship has been the portion of all mankind. No man is exempted; you are either cursed or blessed; there is no neutral ground.

Christ has redeemed us from the curse of the law, having become a curse for us (for it is written, "Cursed is everyone who hangs on a tree"), that the blessing of Abraham might come upon the Gentiles in Christ Jesus, that we might receive the promise of the Spirit through faith GALATIANS 3:13-14

The only way to the covenant of Abraham is through Jesus Christ. You cannot come into this covenant without accepting what Jesus does with His Blood. If you are going to enjoy the blessing you must have active faith in the Blood of Jesus. There is no other option for you except you want to remain under the curse and its effects. No blood, no covenant. The way into the blessing is stained with Blood of the Son of God. Now is the time to apply the Blood by faith.

Jesus took our place, taking upon His head our curse. He destroyed the curse and its effect in His Blood and again man is released to enjoy the blessings of Abraham.

Friends, unlike curse, the blessing is an empowerment to have success, it is God's grace to see increase in all that we do. It is to bring continuous improvement upon us.

Curse, on the other hand, is to cast a spell upon someone or something. It is to bar someone from the benefits due to him. It is setting a man aside for destruction. Jesus broke the curse on our lives of poverty, lack and even debt. The Blood from the crown of thorns that pierced His head reverses the curse eternally. Now the saints can rise up again to enjoy the land that flows with milk and honey. God's divine provision is made available through the Blood.

I boldly declare upon you: NO MORE LACK!

His Hand

For dogs have surrounded Me; The congregation of the wicked has enclosed Me. They pierced My hands and My feet; PSALMS 22:16

The hands of Jesus were pierced through with nails and He bled to break every chain that frustrates all that man lays his hands upon. Praise God. Since Adam sinned, all that man placed his hand upon does not produce to the full strength. The land that once brought enough for man is now barren. Work that was once a pleasure is now with back breaking labour that produces little or nothing.

> *Then to Adam He said, "Because you have heeded the voice of your wife, and have eaten from the tree of which I commanded you, saying, 'You shall not eat of it':"Cursed is the ground for your sake; In toil you shall eat of it All the days of your life. Both thorns and thistles it shall bring forth for you, And you shall eat the herb of the field. In the sweat of your face you shall eat bread Till you return to the ground, For out of it you were taken; For dust you are, And to dust you shall return*
> GENESIS 3:17-19

As a result of this curse man's power to create wealth was hindered but for the Blood. The Blood that flows through His hand restored ECONOMIC POWER to you again. Man can now prosper again. Man can now enjoy his work because of the Blood.

His hands were nailed to the cross, to make our hand prosper in all that we do.

Hands also speak of the strength to make

money, or put in a better way: to create wealth. Anything that reduces your strength to make money or put you in a better stead to create wealth is broken when Jesus' hand was nailed to the cross and Blood flowed out. Every curse upon your hands is forever broken and destroyed when Jesus hands were nailed.

I prophesy over you that your hands will prosper.

The Lord will command the blessing on you in your storehouses and in all to which you set your hand, and He will bless you in the land which the Lord your God is giving you
DEUTERONOMY 28:8

For a believer under the Blood, PROSPERITY IS NOT IN THE FUTURE. Prosperity is now to be received by faith in His word. Make a bold declaration with me: The Blood has been applied; EVERYTHING that I touch and do shall PROSPER.

Listen, because of the Blood that flows through Jesus' hand, your business will prosper. No more curse on your business. Let me say more boldly: by the Blood that flows from Jesus' hand CURSE IS BROKEN OFF YOUR FINANCES. Your business is blessed;

all that you touch are blessed. The power of debt is broken over you because of what the Blood has done. If you are a believer, the Blood will work FOR YOU. Shout: I believe!

His Feet

Every place on which the sole of your foot treads shall be yours: from the wilderness and Lebanon, from the river, the River Euphrates, even to the Western Sea, shall be your territory
DEUTERONOMY 11:24

Jesus' pierced feet reposition man for his dominion mandate. Man strayed from his mandate in the garden. From then man became a subject to the devil. The feet of man are not glorious as it used to be in the garden. All that man once rules now control and dominate him. Man is not fit to carry on his assignment from that point.

Listen, no man clothed in defeat is qualified to carry the glorious gospel to the dying world. What God has not done in you , you cannot convince others to accept.

Jesus bled from His feet to empower man to have dominion over all the power of the enemy and his works. Praise God, we have authority by the Blood to enforce the defeat of the enemy and to carry this glorious gospel of liberty to a world in bondage.

Behold, I give you the authority to trample on serpents and scorpions, and over all the power of the enemy, and nothing shall by any means hurt you
LUKE 10:19

Friend, we do not just go places, we take with us the Blood that flows from His feet there. Feet talk of possession; we are taking cities, nations and kingdoms for our King. Feet speak of destiny; now we can rise up again and step into our enviable destiny. You are restored back to your original purpose at creation.

Then God blessed them, and God said to them, "Be fruitful and multiply; fill the earth and subdue it; have dominion over the fish of the sea, over the birds of the air, and over every living thing that moves on the earth
GENESIS 1:28

We run with our feet, it talks of speed and acceleration. We undertake take journey with our feet. Get ready; you are taking a journey to destiny. God is ordering your steps; you are meeting with the right people and the right opportunities. No more delay.

Delay has made many people lost their hope and thereby missed the ultimate harvest.

I break the yoke of delay over your destiny NOW. No surprise the psalmist cried in Psalms 90:14:

Oh, satisfy us early with Your mercy, That we may rejoice and be glad all our days!

Hear me; until Jesus' feet were pierced and He died on the cross man was cursed in his going out and coming in. Praise God, the Blood breaks and destroys the curse; now you can boldly confess it by faith: I am blessed in my going out and blessed in my coming in. Until you walk the walk, the power in the Blood does not work for you.

Blessed shall you be when you come in, and blessed shall you be when you go out DEUTERONOMY 28:6

HIS BACK

But He was wounded for our transgressions, He was bruised for our iniquities; The chastisement for our peace was upon Him, And by His stripes we are healed ISAIAH 53:5

Jesus' body was scourged and broken before and during His crucifixion, When Jesus walked on earth, He was vibrant, and His body was full of life and health. He didn't know sickness in any form until He took man's sin and the effects of sin upon Himself. But before Jesus went to the cross, He was badly scourged by the Roman soldiers and His body was torn as He hung on the cross.

His back endured the stripes needed to bring about our healing. Jesus endured the 39 stripes needed for man's total freedom from ALL sickness and diseases.

Friend, there is no sickness that can escape the Blood.

At the cross, God also took all our sicknesses and diseases, known and yet unknown and put them on Jesus' complete and healthy body, so that we can walk in divine health and long and fulfilled life without sickness or disease.

That is why the Bible says in 1 Peter 2:24:

who Himself bore our sins in His own body on the tree, that we, having died to sins, might live for righteousness — by whose stripes you were healed.

During the recent Ebola outbreak in West Africa that spread to nations, many believed in the power of this deadly virus to spread than the Blood of Jesus to stop it and destroy it. Any time you bow to fear you reject faith and God's only solution. Nothing comes to man from God without the Blood.

Friend, it is time you stop letting fear control your emotion. Instead, let faith in the finished work of Christ be the thing that controls your mouth and emotion. The Blood is perfect to heal the spirit, soul and body of us ALL. It is the Blood that guarantees total freedom from sickness.

Again, I am repeating myself, when the price of healing is too high for medical science the Blood of Jesus will pay it. I know we are going to meet Jesus one day in heaven but we do not have to travel to meet our King in the devil's wagon - sickness is the devil wagon to early grave. As you begin to make your faith in the Blood active, you will see the cloud of sickness over you disappear in Jesus' name.

HIS SIDE

But when they came to Jesus and saw that He was already dead, they did not break His legs. But one of the soldiers pierced His side with a spear, and immediately blood and water came out. JOHN 19:33-34

Praise God, the power of sin is eternally broken. Every man that does not take the benefits that comes from His Blood now remains under the power of sin by choice.

Yes, we can now say the Blood cleanses us from sin, from its guilt and power. The Blood cleanses us of two things: the guilt of sin and the power of sin.

Now, friend, the fountain is flowing; go, wash in the Blood

In that day a fountain shall be opened for the house of David and for the inhabitants of Jerusalem, for sin and for uncleanness. ZECHARIAH 13:1

You do not have to keep paying the price for sin. Jesus already paid it once and for all in His Blood. You are free from sin eternally. You may not have been walking in that reality yet. But legally that is what happens to you when Jesus shed His Blood. He said it is finished. All that you need to be free from sin is done because of the Blood.

*and from Jesus Christ, the faithful
witness, the firstborn from the dead, and
the ruler over the kings of the earth. To
Him who loved us and washed us from
our sins in His own blood,*
REVELATION 1:5

The cord of sin that holds you fast is
broken because of the Blood that He shed
and applied by faith. Only the Blood sets
free from the slavery of sin.

Come on, this is good news to everyone
that is caught by the enemy due to sin.
No man, who actively puts his faith in the
finished work of Christ, can remain under
the supremacy of the power of sin. The
Blood wins where sin once reigned. Once
a man tastes the freedom from sin and its
accompanying pains, he will never want to
live without the Blood for a day. The power
of sin cannot pass beyond the cross. The
cross is how far sin can travel. The Blood
that flows from the side of the Son of God
takes away the power sin has over you
completely.

*His own iniquities entrap the wicked
man, And he is caught in the cords of
his sin.*   PROVERBS 5:22

TAKE BLOOD COVERING NOW

Arise, shine; For your light has come!
And the glory of the Lord is risen upon
you. For behold, the darkness shall
cover the earth, And deep darkness the
people; But the Lord will arise over
you, And His glory will be seen upon
you   ISAIAH 60:1-2

Danger is coming upon the earth, yes, gross darkness upon the people. The proud and disobedient children are about to be humbled. Only the man under the Blood of Jesus will be saved. If you are not Blood bought you are prone to danger.

The only way to the ark of safety from all forms of evil is through the precious Blood of Jesus. The Lord is coming again. God will once again pass through the land and strike, with an eternal judgment, all who do not have the sign of the Blood. But He will pass over all who drink of the Blood of the New Covenant and eat of the Bread of life.

Then Jesus said unto them, Verily,
verily, I say unto you, Except ye eat the
flesh of the Son of man, and drink his
blood, ye have no life in you
                    JOHN 6:53

And in like manner, He took the cup after supper, saying, This cup is the new testament or covenant [ratified] in My blood, which is shed (poured out) for you
LUKE 22:20

The benefit of the Blood is AVAILABLE to ALL but must be accessed by faith. What is given by Grace must be received by faith. The Blood does no one any good until it is received, applied and acted upon.

We do not enjoy what the word says; it is done for us because of the Blood. The Blood of Jesus guarantees victory on every circumstance. The life of Jesus is in His Blood. This life carrying Blood must be applied by faith. Only faith in the Blood makes you to enjoy what God has made available to you through the Blood.

Whom God hath set forth to be a propitiation through faith in his blood
ROMANS 3 : 25 KJV

The benefits are there but they do us little good unless we apply them. The bible says:

For unto us was the gospel preached as well as unto them; but the word preached did not profit them, not being

mixed with faith in them that heard it
HEBREWS 4:2

Applying the Blood without faith leaves you with man's tradition. Tradition will always make the word of God ineffective. The Blood does not produce in an environment void of faith. Until faith in the Blood is active the Blood remains ineffective.

Thus you have made the commandment of God of no effect by your tradition.
MATTHEW 16: 6

The Blood produces as we take advantage of it by faith only. Apply faith to the good news you hear from this message.

FAITH MIXED WITH CONFESSION

Our Compassionate High Priest Seeing then that we have a great High Priest who has passed through the heavens, Jesus the Son of God, let us hold fast our confession. HEBREWS 4:14

Friend, now let us begin to take full advantage of ALL that the Blood provides. All the benefits of the Blood are here now for receiving. As long as the blood was left in the basin, it was of no effect; it was merely blood that had been shed. The blood had power to save only when it was lifted out of the basin and sprinkled!

How do I sprinkle the Blood upon my life?

And you shall take a bunch of hyssop, dip it in the blood that is in the basin, and strike the lintel and the two doorposts with the blood that is in the basin. And none of you shall go out of the door of his house until morning.
EXODUS 12:22

The shed Blood brings our forgiveness but the Blood will have to be sprinkled to protect and to deliver from all manners of evil.

The head of every family in Israel were to take a bunch of hyssop to sprinkle the blood on the doorposts. The blood in the basin did not do anyone any good until it was sprinkled. That night, when the death angel came and saw the blood on the door posts, he passed over the house. Nothing that destroys can stand a drop of the Blood of Jesus. Until the Blood is applied it remains a religious tradition that lacks the power to set free. Hyssop is a plant used for medicinal and religious purposes.

Praise God, today the new creation in Christ does not have to look for hyssop leaves to apply the Blood. We NOW use our mouth to apply the Blood.

Friend, now you CAN open your mouth to sprinkle ALL things with the Blood of Jesus. When we confess the Word of God we are sprinkling ourselves with the Blood. When you declare:

"The Lord will keep you safe from secret traps and deadly diseases (Psalms 91:3 CEVUK00), you are applying the Blood to protect you from disease and sickness around you.

WHEN YOU BOLDLY CONFESS

And you won't fear diseases that strike in the dark or sudden disaster at mid-day PSALMS 91:6 CEV

The destroyer cannot come near you. The Blood will protect and preserve BOTH the living and non-living things.

Look at this New Testament scripture in Hebrews 9:19:

For when Moses had spoken every precept to all the people according to

the law, he took the blood of calves and goats, with water, scarlet wool, and hyssop, and sprinkled both the book itself and all the people,

Listen because of your position in Christ you have UNLIMITED ACCESS to the life that is running in the Blood of Jesus. All that the Blood offers is yours by FAITH. If it's yours by faith then it must be spoken for you to enjoy it.

Many times believers lay hold on a spiritual truth by faith but they quickly destroy the outcome of their faith by the words that proceed from their mouth. What we believe in our heart must find expression through our mouth. Man creates the reality of his faith by his confession.

Faith that is not confessed is in effective. We need to confess all that the Blood has done, it is doing and will do for us with our mouth. When we confess God's word with our mouth, God will watch over it to perform it. When you confess what the word says, you are realising the life in the Blood to work for you.

When you need to appropriate all that was purchased for us by the Blood then you must sprinkle the Blood with your mouth confessing what is ours in Christ Jesus. Friend, your benefits in the Blood must be preached. The gospel preached must be accepted and believed in our hearts. You then confess what you believe in your heart that is what brings us ALL the blessings that is our portion in Christ. You can never enjoy the benefits in the Blood beyond your confession.

Do not just love the Blood, applied the Blood. Faith is of the heart, you must put your faith in the life hidden in the Blood, and confess what you believe with your mouth then it will bring you the desire victory will come -

Romans 10:10"

For with the heart one believes unto righteousness, and with the mouth confession is made unto salvation."

The life in the Blood is full of power but it will do you no good without your faith. It fakes your faith to make the life in the Blood work for you. It takes your faith to walk in the benefits of the Blood.

It takes faith to release the power of God in your life. We received the Blood by faith we applied the Blood by confessing what the

Blood has done and made available to us.

Friend, as you confess what is yours because of the Blood, you are telling the devil: 'your dominion over me is ended'.

You are denying sickness, whichever name it is given, the right to reign over you. You are breaking the backbone of hardship in Jesus' name. You are choosing prosperity over lack. Hold fast to the confession of what Christ has for you, and then it will become what Christ has done in you. We confess Jesus as Saviour and Lord we become a new creature. Sin loses its grip over us at our confession. Sickness and disease lose their power as we confess the Blood.

Sing the Blood, confess the Blood, Please the Blood and take a cover under the Blood. No devil in hell can stand the Blood. As you confess the Blood by faith the yoke of the enemy is destroyed in your life in Jesus' name.

Friend, as you confess the word, the life that is in the Blood is let loose to destroy the work of death in your body. The Word through man's mouth will establish the dominion of the Spirit of life over the spirit of death.

For the law of the Spirit of life in Christ Jesus has made me free from the law of sin and death ROMANS 8:2

Come, praise God. The word of God in your mouth will destroy every work of evil and put you at the winning side always. The Blood did it ALL - sin-free, disease-free, poverty-free life is in Your blood.

SONGS OF DELIVERANCE

You are my hiding place; You shall preserve me from trouble; You shall surround me with songs of deliverance.
PSALMS 32:7

No man can rise above his confession. The Blood of Jesus is the basis of our victory. But we have to add our testimony, our confession, to it. When we sing we are confessing our faith or fear in something. Singing about the Blood and all that is ours by redemption is releasing our faith to see it manifest in our lives.

Friend, singing about the Blood opens you up for ALL that the Blood paid for on your behalf. As you sing your faith rises up to lay hold of your inheritance in Christ. Everyone benefits singing the Blood except the devil. We have something worth singing about.

We sing our faith in the Blood. Song is a vital part of a sprinkling the Blood in faith. We can go ahead and sing praise to God now because the price for our healing is paid for in His Blood.

Faith in the finished work of Christ is the victory that overcomes; praise is the voice of living faith. Sing the Blood until your trial turns to testimony; sing the Blood until the grip of sickness is loosens over you. Sing the Blood until you are not under the burden of lack anymore.

And they overcame him by the blood of the Lamb and by the word of their testimony, and they did not love their lives to the death. REVELATION 12:11

Let your song reveals the value and virtue in the Blood. As you sing the Blood loud and bold every of your tear is dried now in Jesus' name. Faith comes by hearing, as you sing and hear about the power in the Blood to set free and to deliver words in these songs is sure to release the power of God in your life. Jesus' shed blood purchased our deliverance from the works of Satan.

Sing your benefit in the Blood out loud NOW and see your Breakthrough manifest. The Blood is applied through faith in our speaking and singing. We overcome by the Blood, as it is the word of our testimony. We testify as to its necessity and as to its sufficiency to meet all needs at all times.

I will sing with the spirit, and I will also sing with the understanding
1 CORINTHIANS 14: 15

Chapter Four

As long as we carry the word of God and the Blood on our lips we will always have a hope and future no matter what is happening in the world.

- KOLA O. EMIOLA -

Access Granted

Then, behold, the veil of the temple was torn in two from top to bottom; and the earth quaked, and the rocks were split, and the graves were opened; and many bodies of the saints who had fallen asleep were raised; and coming out of the graves after His resurrection, they went into the holy city and appeared to many　　　MATTHEW 27:51-54

SO **when the centurion and those with him, who were guarding Jesus, saw the earthquake and** the things that had happened, they feared greatly, saying: Truly this was the Son of God!

So when Jesus had received the sour wine, He said, "It is finished!" And bowing His head, He gave up His spirit.　　　JOHN 19:30

Much of the weakness of the Church is due to its failure to understand and take advantage of this all-important truth and all the benefits that come through the Blood.

Everything a believer needs to enjoy the best life has been provided for and made accessible by the Blood. You can NOW take hold of all that you are and you have in Christ Jesus by faith through the Blood. All came through the Blood. Jesus said it is finished, implying that 'I have done all I need to do and will ever do to give you access to all of God'.

Our access to God and our inheritance in Christ is through the Blood. Friend, there is no going around the Blood to access what is yours in Christ. If you must enjoy any benefit in Christ you must accept to come through the Blood. You cannot want life apart from the Blood of Christ. When Jesus shed His Blood He destroyed all excuses man has to give for failing. You have no reason to remain captive to addiction; your excuses are not strong enough to remain a crown victim of life. The Blood has been applied. NOW you can go for the best life in Christ if you so desire.

Access simply means the ability, right, or permission to approach, enter, speak with, or use something.

ACCESS TO OUR FATHER GOD

Hold Fast Your Confession Therefore, brethren, having boldness to enter the Holiest by the blood of Jesus,
      HEBREWS 10:19

But now in Christ Jesus you who once were far off have been brought near by the blood of Christ. For He Himself is our peace, who has made both one, and has broken down the middle wall of separation   EPHESIANS 2:13-14

Our access to God is through the Blood. The Blood carries us into the Holy of Holies. The Blood causes God to deliver us from judgment due to man. It was a lamb for a household (Exodus 12), and Jesus is the Lamb of God that takes away the sins of the world. We can now come to God's presence boldly without any fear.

The Blood is the end of the cry for power, peace, victory and all good gifts that come from the presence of our Father – God. They pray. There is only one way to access the throne of glory. It is 'through the Blood'.

Friend, no man can come to the presence of God without the Blood. Nothing comes from the presence of God to man without the Blood.

Every good gift and every perfect gift is from above, and comes down from the Father of lights, with whom there is no variation or shadow of turning.
JAMES 1:17

We have access to our Father- God and all that we need now and will ever need through the Blood only. No more wall of separation, we are now joint heir with Jesus Himself.

Listen friend, we have common inheritance with Jesus. Why? This is because we have the same Father. By the Blood Jesus has reconciled us back to our Father.

ACCESS TO RIGHTEOUSNESS

For if by the one man's offense death reigned through the one, much more those who receive abundance of grace and of the gift of righteousness will reign in life through the One, Jesus Christ ROMANS 5:17

The Blood brings to an end all condemnation. Man's striving to earn God's approval ceased when Jesus shed His Blood. This happens when we allow the word and the Blood to do their work on us. We accept the word we hear in faith and allow the Blood to wash us from sin, and then we have eternal life.

Friend, righteousness is imparted immediately into our spirit. This is how far the power of sin can work in your life. You were a sinner saved by grace but now you are the Righteousness of God. You are now in the same class with Jesus .This opens us to our royal state. Slavery has come to an end. Where sin stopped, slavery ends.

Man was never designed for slavery. When you become born again, you are not a part of God and part of Satan. You become all of God. Satan has no claim to God's righteousness any longer. You belong to God. You are God's righteousness.

For He made Him who knew no sin to be sin for us, that we might become the righteousness of God in Hm.
2 CORINTHIANS 5:21

Righteousness is God's free gift Jesus gave when He shed His Blood on the cross for all. When a man becomes a new creature, the same moment he received the righteousness of God that comes with some divine privileges, rights and freedom. You may not take advantage of what is yours right by your right- standing with God but it is there for you in the store always.

Satan has no right to rule you again. Now step into your reigning state. You have right to everything that God has. No, you are not begging for it, it is yours to be enjoyed. All things are yours NOW.

ACCESS TO GRACE AND GLORY

through whom also we have access by faith into this grace in which we stand, and rejoice in hope of the glory of God.
ROMANS 5:2

Everything provided in Christ must be accessed by faith. Yes it is given but it must be received only by faith. The Blood opens us up to this life of grace. Paul says this grace, what is this particular grace? It is the freedom we now have in Christ. It is the liberty to enforce heaven on earth. This is our experience now, not only in the hereafter.

Praise God, we have access to our Father, God. That is not enough; we also enjoy access to this grace. This is grace that has become our lifestyle.

Friend, this life of grace does not stop when we become new in Christ, it only marks the beginning. Now through the finished work of Christ we have complete access to freedom. Now we can shout: Freedom Reigns!

We are standing our ground in this freedom. Come on, the life Jesus bought for us with His Blood is better than the life Adam lost through disobedience in the garden.

I like the way the Complete Jewish Version (CJW) of the Bible put the above verse:

Also through him and on the ground of our trust, we have gained access to this grace in which we stand; so let us boast about the hope of experiencing God's glory ROMANS 5:2

We can now shout and let the whole world knows that we are experiencing a lifestyle of grace and glory now and forever.

When Adam sinned man fell short of the glory of God but when the Blood of Jesus was shed and sprinkled by faith man began to experience the glory of God again. There is no shortage of glory now. We all can daily experience grace and glory. You cannot be in His presence without experiencing the glory of His presence.

ACCESS TO ETERNAL LIFE

Then Jesus said to them, "Most assuredly, I say to you, unless you eat the flesh of the Son of Man and drink His blood, you have no life in you. Whoever eats My flesh and drinks My blood has eternal life, and I will raise him up at the last day. For My flesh is food indeed, and My blood is drink indeed. He who eats My flesh and drinks My blood abides in Me, and I in him.

JOHN 6:53-56

The word and the Blood must have their works in man for him to have life. This is not just ordinary human life. The life in the above scripture means God's kind of life. In Greek it is called 'Zoe'. Jesus made it so clear why He came in John 10:10:

I have come that they may have life, and that they may have it more abundantly.

This is the life that puts you in the same class like God. This is the nature of God imparted to man at the new creation. This is the part of man that communicates with God. This new creation is not a new denomination. No, it is not an improved man. It is not a place where we have been taught the wrong doctrine. Rather, it is the life of God in you that makes you become the light of your generation.

In Him was life, and the life was the light of men. John 1:4

We have eternal life NOW, it is not a matter that will be settled in the future. It is not what you have gradually. It is instant. You hear the word and believe what you hear about the finished work of Christ and allow the Blood to wash you. Now we have eternal life.

Friend, we are back to the Father's presence because of the Blood. Eternal life in His presence is NOW. This life always comes with side effects. The eternal life of God will have an effect on your life, habits, and the quality of life you now live. Eternal life, when fully in operation, has impact on your physical body. Spiritual death gave man physical death or mortality for his body. But the new birth gives eternal life to the spirit of man now and the promise of immortality for our physical bodies at the return of the Lord Jesus Christ, the only Lamb of God.

always carrying about in the body the dying of the Lord Jesus, that the life of Jesus also may be manifested in our body. 2 Corinthians 4:10

Now that we have eternal life within us the power of the spirit of life destroys the spirit of death. Healing is made available now for our mortal bodies. It is God's nature that makes man the master; life as it was in the beginning. This life that lightens every man must be walked in to profit anyone. No man who has the eternal life calls the Blood of Jesus common.

Friend, this eternal life is what makes the new creature an heir of God and joint heir with Christ.

> *and if children, then heirs — heirs of God and joint heirs with Christ,*
> ROMANS 8:17

We are free from satanic harassment just the same way Jesus was free from his control and rule. Again, we are as free as Jesus was free from the rulership of Satan.

ACCESS TO THE THRONE

> *To Him who loved us and washed us from our sins in His own blood, and has made us kings and priests to His God and Father, to Him be glory and dominion forever and ever. Amen.*
> REVELATION 1:5 -6

The access back into our dominion mandate is again open as we allow the Blood to wash us from our sins. Your covenant rulership is made possible as we lay hold on what the Blood has done for us and in fact is doing in us now. Until we appreciate the shed Blood, dominion remains a dream. We are accepted by God to reign as kings in the affairs of life.

You are now open to royalty because the Blood has been shed. There is an unbreakable link between the shed Blood and your kingship. The gate back to life as it was in Eden is the way of the Blood. Now we can choose to have life full of 'honey' in Christ.

Friend, we believers sometimes know and understand how to take our place as soldiers of Christ but we have little understanding on our kingship. Soldiers always think of the next battle. Kings think about reigning. Soldiers talk warfare, kings celebrate victory. Soldiers obey and fight, kings rule and reign. Kings decree what they desire to see. History remembers kings not soldiers.

By me kings reign, And rulers decree justice.   PROVERBS 8:15

Jesus' DNA is in you by your new birth, royalty runs all through your blood. Get up and take your place, reigning in all affairs of life. Listen, when an unbeliever takes a lead in our sphere of life it is because the believer is yet to take his place as king. Our dominion mandate covers every sphere of life and society. When the Blood was shed Jesus became our wisdom.

Kings reign by wisdom; soldiers think of weapons of war. It is time to display the wisdom from above to this generation.

Wisdom is better than weapons of war;
But one sinner destroys much good.
ECCLESIASTES 9:18

The Blood is not only a weapon of war against the enemy, it is also an access to our reigning in life. The Son of God became incarnate, not merely that He might save men from their sins, but also that He might bring man to that place of dominion and reigning. Accept your reigning seat, and begin to exercise the spiritual authority which it confers upon you. It is your honour. And it is time you are comfortable with reigning. Royal welcome awaits you in every turn.

To bind their kings with chains, And their nobles with fetters of iron; To execute on them the written judgment—This honor have all His saints. Praise the Lord!   PSALMS 149:8-9

Friend, come on, let us manifest the dignity of a member of the royal household of heaven here on earth.

each one resembled the son of a king.
JUDGES 8: 18

ACCESS TO SANCTIFICATION

Of how much worse punishment, do you suppose, will he be thought worthy who has trampled the Son of God underfoot, counted the blood of the covenant by which he was sanctified a common thing, and insulted the Spirit of grace?   HEBREWS 10:29

But of Him you are in Christ Jesus, who became for us wisdom from God — and righteousness and sanctification and redemption   1 CORINTHIANS 1:30

Righteousness is the nature of God in you imparted into a new creature. Holiness is your conduct of a new creation. We do not grow in our   Righteousness. We do grow in our knowledge of our Righteousness and our rights and privileges as God's righteousness in Christ. But we do grow in holiness and mature more in our character.

When you become born again your spirit man becomes sanctified. But your mind needs to be continually renewed for it to be in submission to your spirit. Your spirit always agrees with the word of God. Your mind is not always in agreement with the word of God. Your body goes in the direction of your mind.

Man's spirit is designed to have dominion over his mind and when that happens the body listens to the dictates of the mind. Until a man's spirit is sanctified it is impossible for him to live a life of holiness. A holy mind makes a believer to present his body as a living sacrifice unto God. A sanctified spirit leads to holy living. Jesus has become our wisdom. Jesus is our Righteousness and He is our sanctification. We are holy as we remain in our position in Christ.

> *to those who are sanctified in Christ Jesus, called to be saints, with all who in every place call on the name of Jesus Christ our Lord, both theirs and ours*
> I CORINTHIANS 1:2

ACCESS TO ALL ROUND VICTORY

Now I saw heaven opened, and behold, a white horse. And He who sat on him was called Faithful and True, and in

righteousness He judges and makes war. His eyes were like a flame of fire, and on His head were many crowns. He had a name written that no one knew except Himself. He was clothed with a robe dipped in blood, and His name is called The Word of God.
REVELATION 19:11-13

No Blood washed child of God should live a life of defeat any more. To be Blood sprinkled is to be power wrapped. Our deliverance is a settled matter; all we do now is enforcing the victory purchased for us all by the Blood.

Friend, as long as we carry the word of God and the Blood on our lips we will always have a hope and future no matter what is happening in the world. We have all the abilities to win battles because Jesus won 'the war'. Until a man puts his faith to action he remains the same and his situation remains unchanged.

If the life in the Blood cannot destroy this life threatening sickness there is no assurance that the Blood can set you free from the power of sin. If the Blood cannot break the backbone of hardship over your life why trust the Blood for cleansing? The Blood of Jesus sets free from sin and all that accompany sin so that we can enjoy all that accompany our salvation.

Praise God we are victors! Jesus has won the victory for us; His Blood has prevailed. And all we need to do now is to enforce our victory because of the Blood.

Now we declare:

The Blood of Jesus sets free from sin and all that accompany sin so that we can enjoy all that accompany our salvation.

I proclaim the victory of the Blood of Jesus! I am Blood-washed, Blood-bought, Blood-justified, Blood-saved, and Blood-ransomed. And I proclaim the victory of the Blood of Jesus!

No more defeat, the Blood has prevailed.

Friend, rise, take all that God has made available to us through the Blood and stop the enemy at the gate! Shalom.

KOLA O. EMIOLA

Chapter Five

....

As a believer we have a mandate to repeat the story of God's love and power to this unsettled world.

- Kola O. Emiola -

Here are the proofs

FRIEND your testimony is announcing the good news of Jesus to the whole world. Testimony is what another man has experience and made possible to you.

> *The law of the Lord is perfect, convert-ing the soul; The testimony of the Lord is sure, making wise the simple;*
> PSALMS 19:7

Testimonies are the stories of the faithfulness of God in the life of believers. Testimonies are the open declaration that the word is true in the mouth of the man who is a doer of the word. Testimonies are also proof of the believer's firsthand experience and enjoyment of the benefits of the word in his life. Testimonies are faith booster.

Testimony is the sustaining power of every believer that consistently walks in victory. They carry with them the ability to reproduce same in the life of everyone who will put their faith in the finished work of Christ into action. If God did it in the past He can repeat it again now. It can happen to you too and become a blessing to your world.

As a believer we have a mandate to repeat the story of God's love and power to this unsettled world.

Here are the doings of our Father, alone. The word wins, the Blood wins always. Always effective in working

MIRACLE CONCEPTION

HSG test result showed negative. The medical report was that the fallopian tube was blocked indicating that my wife cannot carry a baby. Flushing was recommended by the doctor. I dropped the scan result on the altar, Papa prayed for us saying that it was a doctor's report. He went on building our faith more about the redemptive power in the blood of Jesus.

We decided to give the money we saved for the flushing of the womb to the offering box. Surprisingly after the prayer Papa prayed, my wife missed her period within 30days. She became pregnant, and just like a joke, the pregnancy was growing. But the doctor was stuck to his evil report and he kept saying the baby would never develop. We held on to God's word from Papa that doctors are not your God; doctors are not your prophet.

We held to the word of God as declared by our prophet. Papa. To the glory of God, here we are today with the baby and mother, hale and healthy.

I really thank God and greatly appreciate our father in the house. God indeed proved that doctors are not our God neither are they our prophet .The Lord confirmed the word of His servant. Praise, praise, praise the Lord.

Engr A.C

DIVINE HEALING THROUGH THE BLOOD

There was this serious itching all around my body for quite some time now. I have applied antibacterial ointments but yet the itching persisted. I kept confessing God's word, the truth about the blood of Jesus as taught by Papa. This fateful Sunday, as Papa was teaching on the mysteries of the blood of Jesus, he referred to a scripture that hit me: Joel 2:21 which says:

> *I will cleanse their blood, the blood of them that I have not yet cleansed.*

He served the Holy Communion and asked us to declare a divine purging and cleansing in every part of our body. So amazing the itching is nowhere to be found in my body again. God is real. God is good. I Praise the name of our God.
Bro G. A

GREAT DELIVERANCE

The God of our father is real. He is a truthful God. He is indeed practical in His doings. For long, I have been having itching round my feet and my body generally. I have not been available for some times now but when I was informed about this programme: the 'Potter's Hands', I got the handbills. I was excited for I knew God would wrought wonders again as usual. It then dawned on me the same hand of the God of my father can do it without waiting for the day of the programme.

With this faith I placed the handbill on my feet and rubbing my body with it saying that the God of Papa Emiola should heal me. Surprisingly the itching stopped, till now and forever in Jesus' name. Praise God with me.

Sis J

MIRACULOUS HEALING

The God of this commission is a miracle working God. A friend of mine was having a running nose continuously. She took drugs but to no avail. She was disturbed because it already was becoming an embarrassment to her. I told her that as medication had failed, God's power would surely prevail. I gave her the handkerchief; the miracle cloth that Papa prayed on during the 'Potter's Hands' programme.

With the belief that the same grace upon Papa has been released upon the miracle cloth for multidimensional act of the Gods' power, I put the miracle cloth on her nose and prayed for her. The running nose stopped, to my surprise. This God is an awesome God.

Dcnes B. T

Accelerated Promotion, Unlimited Breakthrough

What the Lord has done for me has been so amazing that my colleagues always marvel at me. Since I joined the Church after I was asked to go forward (sacked) in my former place of work, the God of our father has been lifting me up, He provided for me a good job. He has been taking me from one level to the other.

By the grace of God what we could not achieve in years God made it possible through the undiluted teaching of God's word in this place. God built a house for us. Also, on the 3rd of January my wife got a letter of transfer to Abeokuta. She was barely six months in the new office when she was promoted to the position of Operation Manager.

In my office there was a series of examinations and screening that we were all subjected to. I was worried that I might be one of those that will be sacked again, I remembered Papa always emphasises that no one will be sacked and that we are the ones that will tender our letter of resignation/retirement at will.

The tension was so high. I thank God I was not sacked but promoted. In fact, I had accelerated promotion and within a year I got increment thrice and my salary was increased by 90%.

There is a unique grace upon our Papa here and the team of our pastors in this ministry. I want to urge you to take all the teachings and instructions given to us in this place very seriously because none of God's word here will ever go unfulfilled.

God is a good God. The lifter of our heads.
Halleluyah. *Bro D.I*

WITCHCRAFT DESTROYED BY THE BLOOD

I thank God. It happened that my daughter cried from the dream and thereafter began to shout 'my leg, my leg'. From then she could not walk or stand. I went to meet Papa in the office and he prayed for the girl. I thank God that right there the girl stood up and walked by herself again. Praise God. *Sis.M.K*

THE WORD WORKS

Hello, you may not remember me but I heard you speak a couple years ago at the Revolution Church in Port Angeles, WA. You spoke about carrying your left overs with you and I can't even begin to tell you how much that impacted my life! Shortly after that I was hospitalised for a triple pulmonary embolism; PE, for short, for four days.

During this time, I never lost hope. Even when the doctor's verdict was that I had less than 30% chance to live, I thanked God that even if it was only 1% chance I had, not to talk of as much as 30%, I would live. While in hospital I was worshipping from my bed, I couldn't walk as the pain was unbearable and I had no family to come and visit me.

I literally laid in worship for four days! Haha! When I was finally discharged from hospital many struggles came because of the ailment, PE. I had to take injected shots twice a day for 24 days. This was seven times longer than normal but my blood would not thin. Even as I was in the hospital, I remembered your teaching about leftovers and decided to take a selfie because I knew that God was not done with me yet and it was not the end of my earthly journey.

I knew I was already healed but just waiting for the doctors to declare it! HA! HA!! Today, in my living room I have a "before and after" pictures! The first picture is of me in the hospital and the 2nd picture is of me two weeks out of the hospital! What a sharp contrast! Praise, prayer, and worship did it for me during this time!

You helped to change my whole outlook on life and gave me an unquenchable drive to see God move in those around me. Fast forward to today, I'm taking a class called Love Says Go online with Jason Chin. It has been amazing to see how God wants to bless the people we come in contact with every day!!!   *J J, Port Angeles, WA*

LIFE RESTORED THROUGH THE MIRACLE CLOTH.

I visited a Muslim family. Getting there I saw that one of the Alhaji' s little son was terribly sick. In fact, life was not visible in him again. I was told that the boy was rejected in the hospital since all medications were ineffective on the boy. Several tests and diagnoses were carried out but to no avail and so the hospital bluntly rejected him. Seeing the boy and hearing about the ordeal I was moved with compassion, then I sought the permission to pray for the boy from the father, who is an Alhaji. I told the family about the miracle cloth from our Church and they consented to its use.

In the presence of everybody I placed the miracle cloth on the boy assuring them that the same grace that is upon my father in the Lord will work through the miracle cloth because he had prayed on the miracle clothes during our Potter's Hand programme. I prayed a simple prayer and to the glory of God the boy sneezed, began to sweat and finally he jacked back to life. Our God is so good. *Sis J*

TWO YEARS BOIL DRIED UP

One of my neighbours, a Muslim lady, had been nursing a boil for about two years now. She used all manners of medication but the case grew worse, according to her. She just opened up to me and showed me this incurable boil looking like a tumor. Well, I told her my God can heal her.

Honestly the sight of it was terrifying. I summoned courage to pray for her, gave her a miracle cloth from the potter's hand. She placed the cloth on the spot of the boil and to our surprise, the boil disappeared before day break. Brethren God is into it and the days of the supernatural are here. Please let's launch out in faith to bring healing, deliverance and total salvation to our generation. Those miracle clothes are indeed carriers of the power of God. God is real and the word truly works. Praise the Lord! *Dcn B.T*

Appendicitis Healed

Praise the Lord. I was told that a friend of mine had been hospitalised for some days. I visited her in the hospital where she explained her painful experiences to me. She had critical appendicitis .She was slated for operation but unfortunately the appendicitis had burst and she continued wallowing in pain and agony day and night. She could not sleep for days because of the pain. It was so bad that she kept saying repeatedly that she wanted to die and was begging me to help beg the doctor to inject her with death injection.

However, I was consistently rebuking her and the spirit of death, declaring that she would live and not die. I remembered I was with the miracle cloth from the Church. I gave it to her to lay it upon herself which she did and I prayed that the God of my Papa should step in and I left. Surprisingly when I got there the following day she told me that for the first time in many days she slept soundly and well. The pain disappeared. She looked and sounded healthy. Also, it was confirmed that she was carrying a three months pregnancy.

Sis J. U

Delivered From Demonic Attack

After the prophetic power service on Sunday, I got home relaxing and meditating on one of the Papa's recent teachings on the scope of the authority of a believer. Suddenly I felt a painful pinch like a bite on my body, not so long all of my body began to swell up with marks appearing on my body. I became weak and dizzying. Before I knew it was turning to another thing then I remembered the message and I began declaring the word as taught by Papa. I asked my wife to bring the miracle cloth and she rubbed my body with it declaring God's word along with me. After some minutes I slept off, to wake up about 20 minutes later. But now I woke up hail and healthy. The crabs and swelling had disappeared. What a mighty good God we serve. Halleluyah!

Pst T.S

Books by:
KOLA O. EMIOLA
Can help you to step into

Breakthrough & Influence and in

all areas:

Other Books Include:

> Breakingforth Into Freedom

> Leading By The Anointing

> The Power of Encouragement